Th

THE WEE BOOK OF IRISH JOKES

by

John William Tuohy

Paddy & Mick were strolling along one day, when they came across a deserted car. They both jumped in, and started checking if everything was in working order. Paddy beeped the horn, "yes that works ok" he says. Then he flicks on his indicator and calls to "Mick, stick you head outta the window and see if it's working"...to which he replied "it is...it isn't...it is...it isn't..."

Paddy is on his final question for a million pound with Chris Tarrent, he has only one life line left....Phone a friend. Paddy calls murphy with the question "Which bird does not make a nest?
A. Sparrow
B. Swallow
C. Blackbird

D. Cuckoo
Murphy answers "Be Jesus its a Cuckoo 100%" and Paddy wins a the million pound!
Afterwards Paddy rings Murphy and says "How the fook did you know that Murph?"
Murphy says "Well Paddy yer thick bastard..it lives in a fooking clock!"

As Paddy entered the house he looked up to see a ceiling 15 feet high.
'Begod,' he said to Mick, 'when you said you were going to knock two rooms into one I didn't think you meant upwards!!'

Paddys wedding night & his new bride is lying naked, legs spread on the bed. She says "You know what I want". . . . .
. . Paddy says "ALL the fuckin bed by the look of it!"

Paddy and Mike had a bit to drink and were bringing their Irish Air passenger plane into land at the airport when they noticed the runway was ridiculously short.
Mike announced over the com to the passengers to hold on and expect a bumpy landing.

Somehow they made the landing okay. Paddy sweating from the tension exclaimed "Mike, can you believe how short this runway is?"
Mike replied "I know! And look how wide it is!"

Two Indians and an Irishman were walking through the woods. All of a sudden one of the Indians ran up a hill to the mouth of a small cave. "Wooooo! Wooooo! Wooooo!" he called into the cave and listened closely until he heard an answering, "Wooooo! Wooooo! Wooooooo! He then tore off his clothes and ran into the cave.
The Irishman was puzzled and asked the remaining Indian what it was all about."Was the other Indian crazy or what?"
The Indian replied "No, It is our custom during mating season when Indian men see cave, they holler 'Wooooo! Wooooo! Wooooo!' into the opening. If they get an answer back, it means there's a beautiful squaw in there waiting for us."
Just then they came upon another cave. The second Indian ran up to the cave, stopped, and hollered, "Wooooo! Wooooo! Wooooo!"
Immediately, there was the answer. "Wooooo! Wooooo! Wooooo!" from deep inside. He also tore off his clothes and ran into the opening.
The Irishman wandered around in the woods alone for a while, and then spied a third large cave. As he looked in amazement at the size of the huge

opening, he was thinking, " Look at the size of this cave! It is bigger than those the Indians found. There must be some really fine women in this cave!"

He stood in front of the opening and hollered with all his might "Wooooo! Wooooo! Wooooo!"

Like the others, he then heard an answering call, "WOOOOOOOOO, WOOOOOOOOO WOOOOOOOOO!"

With a gleam in his eye and a smile on his face, he raced into the cave, tearing off his clothes as he ran.

The following day, the headline of the local newspaper read "NAKED IRISHMAN RUN OVER BY TRAIN"

Two Irish guys are making letter bombs.
Pat say's "Do you think I have put enough explosives in this envelope?"
"dunno" says Mick "open it and see"
"But it will explode" says Pat
Mick says "Don't be effing stupid......it's not addressed to you"

Two Irishmen, Patrick and Michael, were adrift in a lifeboat, following a dramatic escape from a burning freighter. While rummaging through the boat's provisions. Patrick stumbled across an old lamp. Secretly hoping that a genie would appear, he rubbed the lamp vigorously. To the amazement of Patrick, a genie came forth. This particular genie, however, stated that he could only deliver one wish, not the standard three. Without giving much thought to it, Patrick blurted out, "Make the whole ocean into Guiness Beer."

The genie clapped his hands with a deafening crash, and immediately the entire sea turned into the finest brew ever sampled by mortals, simultaneously, the genie vanished. Only the gentle lapping of Guinness on the hull broke the stillness as two men considered their circumstances.

Michael looked disgustedly at Patrick whose wish had been granted. After a long, tension- filled moment, he spoke: "Nice going, Patrick. Now we're going to have to pee in the boat."

Paddy gets a job felling trees up North. At the end of his first day, the foreman comes to check on his work. Paddy has felled only one tree. "What the hell's going on here, Paddy? Only one tree felled in a day." Paddy says, "This bloody saw's no good, boss. Doesn't cut at all." The boss says, "Here, give us a try." He starts up the chainsaw. Paddy looks startled. "What's that noise, boss?"

An Irishman, an Englishman and a Scotsman are marooned on a desert island. One day they find a curious lamp on the shore. When they rub the lamp a genie appears. He is so grateful for his release, he offers the group 3 wishes, The Englishman wishes to be back in his local pub in Essex. Whoosh - he's gone. The Scotsman wants to be having a pint with his mates in Glasgow. Whoosh - he's gone. The Irishman looks dejected. 'What's the matter?' asks the genie. "Sure it's awful lonely here without my two friends. I wish they were still here." And whoosh - they were.

There is an international beer conference. After a full day of meetings and workshops, three beer representatives go out for a drink. The waiter asks the Miller rep what he wants. He say, "Give me a Miller High Life."
The waiter asks the Budweiser rep what he wants. He says, "Give me a Bud Lite."
Then the waiter asks the Guinness rep what he wants. "I'll have a Diet Coke."
When the waiter leaves, the two reps ask the Guinness guy why he ordered a Coke.
"Well," says the Irishman, "I thought I'd avoid a beer since neither of you was having one."

An old handicapped man lived in the countryside of Northern Ireland and had only one relative, a son. The son was in prison for revolutionary activities.

The father wrote the son. "Now that you're in prison, I have no one to dig up my garden. How can I plant my potatoes if I can't dig up my garden?" The son wrote back: "Don't dig up the garden; that's where I've buried all the guns."

The next day a troop of British soldiers descended on the farm and turned up all the soil. When they found nothing, the old man was confused. He wrote his son: "What's going on? There were no guns." The son wrote back: "Just plant your potatoes."

The parish priest stops Brian on the street and asks how he managed to get so drunk the night before.

"Well, Father," says Brian. "I won a bottle of whiskey in a raffle, and then I fell in with some bad company."

"Bad company? Weren't you with Jim Murphy, Aedan Clark, and Sean Joyce?"

"Yes, father. Bad company."

"Brian, not one of those men drinks."

"Yes, father. That's what I mean. Bad company."

The bishop of Dublin gave a rousing speech on the virtues of marriage. Afterwards, Mary Healey is leaving with her friend Peggy Donogue, mothers of a combined total of 17 children.

"The bishop gave a great sermon," says Mary.

"Ay," says Peggy. "Marriage is a great institution. The bishop said that rightly."

"Ay, he did do that," says Mary, "and I'm thinking I wish I knew as little about the matter as the bishop does."

"Yes," says Peggy, "it was a good sermon."

"Yes," says Mary, "A good sermon. It might be his best ever."

Officer Murphy was called upon to talk down a suicidal jumper on the seventh floor ledge of the Copley Plaza.

Murphy arrives and sticks his head out the window to grab the attention of the jumper.

"Don't jump. For the love of your parents, don't jump."

The young man says, "Actually, I'm an orphan."

"Okay," says Murphy. "Don't jump for the love of your wife or girlfriend."

"I have neither a wife nor a girlfriend," says the jumper.

"Okay," says Murphy, "then don't jump for the love of the saints of Ireland."

The young jumper says, "But I'm not Irish. I'm British."

Murphy says, "Jump, you swine, jump."

Two Irishmen find themselves as patients in the same hospital room. One of them, Dennehy, is completely covered in bandages. The other asks Dennehy, "What happened to you?"

And Dennehy says, "I was comin' outta the bar, and as I stepped into the street, I got hit by a truck. The blow was so fierce, it sent me back into the bar, but through the plate glass window."

"Lucky you," says the other Irishman.

"How do you figure that?" says Dennehy.

"Lucky you because you were covered in all them bandages. Otherwise, you would've been cut to ribbons."

Mickey was a young man from Kerry who only recently had developed a large taste for the drink. After a few nights of carousing, he was stopped on the street by the priest.

"Don't you know, Mickey, you should stop the drinking? If you continue, you'll get smaller and smaller and smaller until you turn into a mouse."

This story frightened the superstitious Irishman. He went home to his Mother and said,

"Hey, ma, if you notice me gettin' smaller and smaller, will you kill the farkin cat!"

One day a priest was walking in Dublin, and he encountered a Protestant minister. They chatted for a while and then the minister invited the priest to his home for a cup of tea. When they got to the minister's home, the priest noticed how shabby the outside was. Inside, the priest noticed how run down the place seemed to be. Then the minister introduced the priest to his wife.

"Father O'Neill," said the minister, "I'd like you to meet my better half."

And so the minister's missus then made them tea. A few days later, the two clergymen met each other again. This time, they went to the priest's rectory, which was a fancy well-appointed Georgian mansion. The minister was very impressed. The priest led him to the kitchen. where he began to make the tea. The kitchen, too, was set up with all the modern conveniences. Finally the minister commented on the wonderful housing the priest had.

"Well," said Father O'Neill, "Here in Ireland, the Protestant ministers have the better halves, but the Catholic priests have the better quarters."

Mary Clancy goes up to Father O' Grady after his Sunday morning service, and she's in tears.

He says, "So what's bothering you, Mary my dear?"

She says, "Oh, Father, I've got terrible news. My husband passed away last night."

The priest says, "Oh, Mary, that's terrible. Tell me, Mary, did he have any last requests?"

She says, "That he did, Father." The priest says, "What did he ask, Mary?"

She says, He said, 'Please Mary, put down that damn gun...'

An Irishman who had a little too much to drink is driving home from the city one night and, of course, his car is weaving violently all over the road.

A cop pulls him over.

"So," says the cop to the driver, where have ya been?"

"Why, I've been to the pub of course," slurs the drunk.

"Well," says the cop, "it looks like you've had quite a few to drink this evening."

"I did all right," the drunk says with a smile.

"Did you know," says the cop, standing straight and folding his arms across his chest,

"That a few intersections back, your wife fell out of your car?"

"Oh, thank heavens," sighs the drunk.

"For a minute there, I thought I'd gone deaf."

A fellow wanted to have his house renovated, but thought that all the estimates he received were too high. Finally he consulted an Irish building contractor who came to view his house.

"I'll completely redecorate your bedroom for £15," said the Irishman.

"Great!" said the fellow, "all the others wanted at least £100."

At this the Irishman rushed over to the window and shouted out, "Green side up, green side up!"

"How about the bathroom?" asked the fellow, "The others wanted at least £250."

"My men and I will do it for £40." said the Irishman, whereupon he rushed to the window and shouted, "Green side up, green side up!"

"Well, you seem to be the man I've been looking for." said the fellow, "Just tell me one thing, why do you go to the window and shout, 'Green side up, green side up'?"

"That's just technical information to my workmen," said the Irishman, "They're laying a lawn next door."

Five Catholic friends were enjoying a coffee in a bistro after a meal.

The first Catholic man tells his friends, "My son is a priest, when he walks into a room, everyone calls him 'Father'."

The second Catholic man chirps, "My son is a Bishop. When he walks into a room people call him 'Your Grace'."

The third Catholic man says, "My son is a Cardinal. When he enters a room everyone says 'Your Eminence'."

The fourth Catholic man says, "My son is the Pope. When he walks into a room people call him 'Your Holiness'."

Since the lone Catholic woman was sipping her coffee in silence, the four men gave her a look and said, "Well....?"

She proudly replies, "I have a daughter, slim, tall, 38 Double D breasts, 24″ waist and 34″ hips. When she walks into a room, people say, "Oh My God.."

Recently a routine police patrol was parked outside a bar in Donegal Town.

After last call, the officer noticed a man leaving the bar so apparently intoxicated that he could barely walk.

The man stumbled around the car park for a few minutes, with the officer quietly observing.

After what seemed an eternity, in which he tried his keys on five different vehicles, the man managed to find his car and fall into it. He sat there for a few minutes as a number of other patrons left the bar and drove off.

Finally he started the car, switched the wipers on and off; it was a fine, dry summer night, flicked the blinkers on and off a couple of times, honked the horn and then switched on the lights. He moved the vehicle forward a few inches, reversed a little, and then remained still for a few more minutes as some more of the other patrons' vehicles left.

At last, when his when his was the only car left in the parking lot, he pulled out and drove slowly down the road The police officer, having waited patiently all this time, now started up his patrol car, put on the flashing lights and promptly pulled the man over and administered a breathalyser test.

To his amazement, the breathalyser indicated no evidence that the man had consumed any alcohol at all! Dumbfounded, the officer said, 'I'll have to ask you to accompany me to the police station. This breathalyser equipment must be broken.'

'I doubt it,' said Paddy , truly proud of himself. 'Tonight I'm the designated decoy!

An Irish priest is driving down to New York and gets stopped for speeding in Connecticut . The state trooper smells alcohol on the priest's breath and then sees an empty wine bottle on the floor of the car.

He says, 'Sir, have you been drinking?'

'Just water,' says the priest.

The trooper says, 'Then why do I smell wine?'

The priest looks at the bottle and says, 'Good Lord! He's done it again!'

Gallagher opened the morning newspaper and was dumbfounded to read in the obituary column that he had died. He quickly phoned his best friend, Finney. 'Did you see the paper?' asked Gallagher. 'They say I died!!'
'Yes, I saw it!' replied Finney. 'Where are ye callin' from?'

Paddy was in New York. He was patiently waiting and watching the traffic cop on a busy street crossing. The cop stopped the flow of traffic and shouted, 'Okay, pedestrians.' Then he'd allow the traffic to pass. He'd done this several times, and Paddy still stood on the sidewalk. After the cop had shouted, 'Pedestrians!' for the tenth time, Paddy went over to him and said, 'Is it not about time ye let the Catholics across?'

Father Murphy walked into a bar and went up to the first man her found and asked
"Do you want to heaven?'
The man said, 'I do, Father.'

The priest said, 'Then stand over there against the wall.'
Then the priest asked the second man, 'Do you want to go to heaven?'
'Certainly, Father,' the man replied.
'Then stand over there against the wall,' said the priest.
Then Father Murphy walked up to O'Toole and asked, 'Do you want to go to heaven?'
O'Toole said, 'No, I don't Father.'
The priest said, 'I don't believe this. You mean to tell me that when you die you don't want to go to heaven?'
O'Toole said, 'Oh, when I die , yes. I thought you were getting a group together to go right now.'

A man walked into a Dublin bar and saw a friend sitting with an empty glass. 'Paddy can I buy you another', he asked, to which Paddy replied - 'now what would I be wanting with another empty glass?'"

Mick met paddy in the street and said "Paddy will please draw your bedroom curtains before making love to your wife in the future?"
"Bejaysus, why ?" Asked Paddy

"Because" re[lied Mick "the whole street was laughing when the saw you making love to your wife yesterday"

"The laugh is on them" says Paddy "I wasn't home yesterday"

A married Irishman went into the confessional and said to his priest, 'I almost had an affair with another woman.' The priest said, 'What do you mean, almost?' The Irishman said, 'Well, we got undressed and rubbed together, but then I stopped.' The priest said, 'Rubbing together is the same as putting it in. You're not to see that woman again. For your penance, say five Hail Mary's and put $50 in the poor box.' The Irishman left the confessional, said his prayers, and then walked over to the poor box. He paused for a moment and then started to leave. The priest, who was watching, quickly ran over to him saying, 'I saw that. You didn't put any money in the poor box!' The Irishman replied, 'Yeah, but I rubbed the $50 on the box, and according to you, that's the same as putting it in!'

Three tortoises, Paddy, Jim and Geoff go for a picnic ten miles from where they live it takes them ten days to get there. When they arrive they find they've forgotten the bottle opener. Jim and Geoff ask paddy to fetch it. Paddy says "Hell no, by I get back you'd have eaten all the sandwiches." Jim and Geoff promise not to eat the sandwiches so Paddy agrees to go. Ten days pass and paddy has not returned twenty days pass and he's still not returned. Jim and Geoff are starving but keep thier promise not to eat the sandwiches. Twenty days pass and they say the hell with it we are going to starve if we don't eat. They start to eat the sandwiches and paddy jumps from behind a rock and shouts "I knew it! You bastards wouldn't wait, I'm not going now"

An Irish woman of advanced age visited her physician to ask his advice in reviving her husband's libido.
"What about trying Viagra?" asked the Doctor.
"Not a chance", she said. "He won't even take an aspirin."
"Not a problem," replied the doctor. "Give him an 'Irish Viagra'.
It's when you drop the Viagra tablet into his coffee. He won't even taste it. Give it a try and call me in a week to let me know how things went."
It wasn't a week later when she called the doctor, who directly inquired as to her progress.
The poor dear exclaimed, "Oh, faith, bejaysus and begorrah! T'was horrid! Just terrible, doctor!"

"Really? What happened?" asked the doctor.
"Well, I did as you advised and slipped it in his coffee and the effect was almost immediate. He jumped straight up, with a twinkle in his eye and with his pants a-bulging fiercely! With one swoop of his arm, he sent me cups and tablecloth flying, ripped me clothes to tatters and took me then and there passionately on the tabletop! It was a nightmare, I tell you, an absolute nightmare!"
"Why so terrible?" asked the doctor, "Do you mean the sex your husband provided wasn't good?"
"Feckin jaysus, 'twas the best sex I've had in 25 years! But sure as I'm sitting here, I'll never be able to show me face in Starbucks again!"

Murphy applied for a fermentation operator post at a famous Irish firm based in Dublin. An American applied for the same job and since both applicants had similar qualifications, they were asked to take a test by the Manager. When the results were in, amazingly, both men had only one wrong answer. The manager went to Murphy and said, "Thank you for coming to the interview, but we've decided to give the American the job."
"And why would you be doing that?" Murphy asked "We both got 19 questions correct. This being Ireland and me being Irish surely I should get the job."

"We have made our decision" the manager replied "not on the correct answers, but on the question you missed."
"And just how would one incorrect answer be better than the other?" Murphy asked
"Simple." the manager said "On question number 7 the American wrote down, 'I don't know.' " "You put down, "Neither do I."

Patrick goes into a bar, sees a sign that states "All you can drink $10" and says "I'll take two!"

I'm so excited. I've just made up my very own Irish joke. It goes like this: An Irish man walks OUT of a bar.

An Irish cop is walking his beat one day when he looks up and sees a man on the ledge of his building getting ready to jump. The cop tries to talk him down, "Young man, think of all the people that care for you, what about your mother?" The man replies, "I was an orphan, copper!". The cop still won't give up, he says "Young man, think of your girlfriend or wife, surely they must care for you?" The man replies "I haven't had a date since my wife ran off with my best friend!" By this time the cop is getting desperate and gives it one last shot. "Young man, won't you please think of the Virgin Mary?" To which the young man replied, "Who?" The cop says, "JUMP YOU LOUSEY PROTESTANT!"

 An Irish man goes into the restroom and at the urinal next to him is a Leprechaun. Wow, he thinks to himself, a Leprechaun! The Leprechaun tells him he can give him three wishes, but only if the man agrees to be sodomized in the bathroom first. Thinking of the great good he could do with his wishes, the Irish man agrees. As the Leprechaun has the Irish man bent over in the stall he asks him how old he is. "43", replies the Irish man amidst his groans of pain. Then the Leprechaun asks him what he does for a living, "I'm a lawyer", cries the Irish man. Then the Leprechaun asks the man if he's married. "Yes, I'm married with 3 children", answers the Irish man. As the Leprechaun finishes his task at hand he says to the man, "Let me get this straight. You're 43 years old, a lawyer, you're married with 3 children and you STILL believe in Leprechauns?"

A young Irish lass was walking toward the confessional when she noticed her friend washing her hands in a basin. Curious she asked "Why be ya washing your hands in the basin?" To which her friend answered "Well I confessed I'd been pleasurin' me boyfriend with me hand last night and now I have to wash it 10 times in the holy water". "Well please try not not get the water too dirty..." said the first. "And why not?" asked her friend. "Well" said the first, "After me confession I think I might be gargling with it!"

An Irishman walks into a bar in Dublin, orders three pints of Guinness and sits in the back of the room, drinking a sip out of each one in turn. When he finishes them, he comes back to the bar and orders three more. The bartender approaches and tells him, "You know, a pint goes flat after I draw it. I think your drinks would taste better if you bought them one at a time." The Irishman replies, "Well, you see, I have two brothers. One is in America, the other is in Australia, and I'm in Dublin. When we all left home, we promised that we'd drink this way to remember the days we drank together. So I drink one for each o'me brothers and one for me self." The bartender admits that this is a nice custom, and leaves it there. The Irishman becomes a regular in the bar, and always drinks the same way: He orders three pints and drinks them in turn. One day, he comes in and orders two pints. All the other regulars take notice and fall silent. When he comes back to the bar for the second round, the bartender says, "I don't want to intrude on your grief, but I wanted to offer my condolences on your loss." The Irishman looks quite puzzled for a moment, then a light dawns in his eye and he laughs. "Oh, no, everybody's just fine," he explains. "It's just that me wife had us join a new Church and I had to quit drinking. Hasn't affected me brothers though.

Paddy asks his wife "will you ever take another man when i die"
" In time,most probably" she replies
"Will you let him sleep in our bed?" asks a forlorn Paddy
"Yes ,in good time i most probably would" she soothes him
"Would you let him play my guitars" enquires a nervous Paddy
"NEVER" implies his wife
"He,s left handed!!!"
Finnegin: Me wife has a terrible habit of staying up 'til two o'clock in the morning. I can't break her of it.
Sean: What on earth is she doin' at that time?
Finnegin: Waitin' for me to come home.

A married Irishman went into the confessional and said to his priest, 'I almost had an affair with another woman.'

The priest said, 'What do you mean, almost?'
The Irishman said, 'Well, we got undressed and rubbed together, but then I stopped.'
The priest said, 'Rubbing together is the same as putting it in. You're not to see that woman again For your penance, say five Hail Mary's and put $50 in the poor box.'
The Irishman left the confessional, said his prayers, and then walked over to the poor box. He paused for a moment and then started to leave.
The priest, who was watching, quickly ran over to him saying, 'I saw that. You didn't put any money in the poor box!'
The Irishman replied, 'Yeah, but I rubbed the $50 on the box, and according to you, that's the same as putting it in!'
Two Irishmen were standing at the base of a flagpole, looking up.
A blonde walks by and asked them what they were doing. Paddy replied, 'We're supposed to be finding the height of this flagpole, but we don't have a ladder.'
The blonde took out an adjustable spanner from her bag, loosened a few bolts and laid the flagpole down.
She got a tape measure out of her pocket, took a few measurements, and announced that it was 18 feet 6 inches.
Then, she walked off.
Mick said to Paddy,

'Isn't that just like a blonde! We Need the height, and she gives us the bloody length.

One day an Irishman, who had been stranded on a deserted island for over 10 years, saw a speck on the horizon. Suddenly there strode from the surf a figure clad in a black wet suit. Putting aside the scuba tanks and mask and zipping down the top of the wet suit stood a drop-dead gorgeous blonde. She walked up to the stunned Irishman and said to him, "Tell me, how long has it been since you've had a good cigar?'
'Ten years,' replied the amazed Irishman.
With that, she reached over and unzipped a waterproof pocket on the left sleeve of her wetsuit and pulled out a fresh package of cigars and a lighter.
He took a cigar, slowly lit it, and took a long drag. 'Faith and begorrah,' said the castaway, 'that is so good! I'd almost forgotten how great a smoke can be!'
'And how long has it been since you've had a drop of good Powers Irish Whiskey?' asked the blonde.
Trembling, the castaway replied, 'Ten years.'
Hearing that, the blonde reached over to her right sleeve, unzipped a pocket there and removed a flask and handed it to him and he took a long happy drink.

Then the woman started to slowly unzip the long front of her wet suit, right down the middle. She looked at the trembling man and asked, 'And how long has it been since you've played around?'
With tears in his eyes, the Irishman fell to his knees and sobbed, 'Jesus, Mary and Joseph! Don't tell me that you've got golf clubs in there too?'

An Irish man, English man and a Scottish man are walking along a beach when they find a lamp. The Scot picks it up, rubs it and out pops a Genie.
Seeing as how there is 3 of them the Genie gives them only 1 wish each.
The scot says 'ok, I want enough money to keep me happy for the rest of my life, so the Genie snaps his fingers and the Scots man has an unlimited bank balance.
The English man says, 'I'm sick of all the foreign bastards coming into my country and taking our women and jobs, I want you to put a big frecking wall around England to no foreign bastards can ever enter England again.
So the Genie snaps his fingers and a wall 1000ft high and 250 ft thick springs up around the whole of England. Nothing can get in or out again.
The Irish man says to the Genie, are you sure that wall around England is strong and NOTHING can escape? The Genie replies, 'absolutely, nothing will

escape'. So the Irish man replies 'ok then, fill the fuck'n thing up with water'.

A boastful Englishman said to an Irishman "take away your friendliness, your wit, your charm and your good looks, your mountains, glens & lochs what have you got?"
"England" replied the Irishman.
During a recent password audit at Bank Of Ireland it was found that Paddy O'Toole was using the following password:"MickeyMinniePlutoHueyLouieDeweyDonald Washington...When asked why he had such a long password, he said " O, I was told it had to be at least 8 characters long and include at least one capital!"

A boastful Englishman said to an Irishman "take away your friendliness, your wit, your charm and your good looks, your mountains, glens & lochs what have you got?"
"England" replied the Irishman.

Two Irishmen working in a field, Paddy is digging holes. Mick is filling them in. After 9 holes, a woman who was passing by asked ' Why are you digging a hole and the other lad filling it in... .'? and Paddy replied 'There's usually three of us, but the lad who plants the trees phoned in sick today'!
"Ireland's worst air disaster occurred early this morning when a small two-seater Cessna plane crashed into a cemetery."...Irish search and rescue workers have recovered 1826 bodies so far and expect that number to climb as digging continues into the night.......

A priest and a nun are on their way back from the cemetery when their car breaks down.

The garage doesn't open until morning so they have to spend the night in a B&B. It only has one room available.

The priest says: "Sister, I don't think the Lord would object if we spend the night sharing this one room. I'll sleep on the sofa and you have the bed."

"I think that would be fine," agrees the nun.

They prepare for bed, say some prayers and settle down to sleep.

Ten minutes pass, and the nun says: "Father, I'm very cold."

"OK," says the priest, "I'll get a blanket from the cupboard."

Another ten minutes pass and the nun says again: "Father, I'm still terribly cold."

The priest says: "Don't worry, I'll get up and fetch you another blanket."

Another ten minutes pass, then the nun murmurs softly: "Father I'm still very cold. I don't think the Lord would mind if we acted as man and wife just for a night."

"You're right," says the priest. "Get your own blankets."

While redecorating a church, three nuns become extremely hot and sweaty in their habits, so Mother Superior says, "Let's take our clothes off, and work naked."

The other two nuns disapprove, and ask, "What if someone sees us?"

But the Mother Superior says, "Don't worry, no one will see us, we'll just lock the door."

So the other nuns agree, strip down and return to work.

Suddenly, they hear a knock at the door, and grab their clothes in a panic.

Mother Superior runs to the door and calls through, "Who is it?"

"Blind man," a man's voice comes back.

So she opens the door, and lets in the blind man, who turns to the nuns and says, "Great tits, ladies, now where do you want these blinds?"

The wise old Mother Superior from county Tipperary was dying. The nuns gathered around her bed trying to make her comfortable. They gave her some warm milk to drink, but she refused it. Then one nun took the glass back to the kitchen. Remembering a bottle of Irish whiskey they had received as a gift the previous Christmas, she opened and poured a generous amount into the warm milk.

When she walked back at Mother Superior's bed, she held the glass to her lips. Mother drank a little, then a little more. Before they knew it, she had drunk the whole glass down to the last drop.

"Mother," the nuns asked with earnest, "please give us some wisdom before you die."

She raised herself up in bed with a pious look on her face and said, "Don't sell that cow."

The bartender was washing his glasses, and an elderly Irishman came in and, with great difficulty, hoisted his bad leg over the barstool, pulled himself up painfully, and asked for a sip of Irish whiskey. The Irishman looked down the bar and said, "Is that Jesus down there?" The bartender nodded, and the Irishman told him to give Jesus an Irish whiskey also.

The next patron was an ailing Italian with a hunched back and slowness of movement. He shuffled up to the barstool and asked for a glass of Chianti. He also looked down the bar and asked if that was Jesus sitting down there. The bartender nodded, and the Italian said to give Him a glass of Chianti, also.

The third patron, a redneck, swaggered in dragging his knuckles on the floor and hollered, "Barkeep, set me up a cold one. Hey, is that God's Boy down there?" The barkeep nodded, and the redneck told him give Jesus a cold one, too.

As Jesus got up to leave, he walked over to the Irishman and touched him and said, "For your kindness, you are healed!" The Irishman felt the strength come back to his leg, and he got up and danced a jig out the door.

Jesus touched the Italian and said, "For your kindness, you are healed!" The Italian felt his back straighten, and he raised his hands above his head and did a flip out the door.

Jesus walked toward the redneck, and the redneck jumped back and exclaimed, "Don't touch me! I'm drawing disability!"

Q: Where does an Irish family go on vacation?
A: A different bar.

First Irish Farmer: "My cow fell down a hole and I had to shoot it."
Second Irish Farmer: "Did you shoot it in the hole?"
First Irish Farmer: " Nope...in the head."

Q: How many Irishmen does it take to screw in a lightbulb?

A: 11 - One to hold the lightbulb, and 10 to drink until the room spins!

How do you sink an Irish submarine?
Knock on the hatch.

An Irish man was stuck on a island for 10 year when all of a sudden he sees a a beautiful woman in a wet suite coming his way. she says what would you like the most in the world right now ? a cigar i haven't smoked in ages. Zips a pocket open and gives him the cigar. Now what? a drink. Zips another pocket down pulls out Irish whiskey. Now let me ask you a question. What? How long has it been since you played around Starts unzipping the middle . Oh sweet mother of pearls don't tell me you have golf clubs in there.

There's this new Irish restaurant being built in downtown Boston. They're going to serve 7-course gourmet Irish meals.

Everyone coming in the door gets a potato and a six pack...

A group of Irish gangsters are sitting around deliberating over methods they will employ in robbing a bank. After a lot of thought they all agree on the way to go about it. In the wee hours of the following morning they meet and embark on their plans to get rich. Once inside the bank, efforts at disabling the internal security system get under way immediately. The robbers expecting to find one or two huge safes filled with cash and valuables were more than surprised to see hundreds of smaller safes scattered strategically through the bank. The first safe's combination was cracked, and inside the robbers found only a bowl of vanilla pudding. "Well," said one robber to another, "at least we got a bit to eat." They open the second safe and it also contained nothing but vanilla pudding, and the process continued until all the safes were opened and there was not one dollar, a diamond, nor an ounce of gold to be found. Instead, all the safes contained containers of pudding.

Disappointed, each of the mobsters made a quiet exit, leaving with nothing more than queasy, uncomfortably full stomachs.

The following morning, a Dublin newspaper headline read: "IRELAND'S LARGEST SPERM BANK ROBBED EARLY THIS MORNING"

St. Peter has a day-off from his duties at the gates to Heaven and Jesus is standing in for him. Whilst 'booking-in' the new arrivals Jesus notices an old man in the queue who seems familiar. When this man gets to the front of the queue Jesus asks him his name.

"Joseph" is the reply, which makes Jesus more inquisitive.

"Occupation?" is the next question, the reply being "Carpenter".

Jesus is now getting quite excited.

In quite a state Jesus asks "Did you have a little boy?", the answer is "yes".

"Did he have holes in his wrists and ankles?" asks Jesus, "Yes" comes the reply. Jesus looks at the old man in front of him and with a tear in his eye shouts "FATHER, FATHER"?!

The old man looks puzzled and after a moment replies.... "Pinnochio?"

An elderly Kerry couple is sitting together watching television. During one of 'those' commercials, the husband asked his wife, "Whatever happened to our sexual relations?" After a long thoughtful silence, the wife replied, "You know, I don't know. I don't even think we got a Christmas card from them this year.

Mick & Paddy are reading head stones at a nearby cemetery. Mick say "Crikey! There's a bloke here who was 152!" Paddy asks "What was his name?" Mick replies "Miles from London!"

Paddy & his wife are lying in bed and the neighbour's dog is barking like mad in the next door garden. Paddy says "To hell with this!" and storms off. He returns five minutes later and the dog is still barking and his wife asks "What did you do?" Paddy replies "I've put the dog in our garden, let's see how they like it!"

A man comes home early and finds Murphy naked, hiding behind the shower curtain.
"What are you doing in there?"
"Voting." Murphy says

In London a homeless Irishman walks up to a proper Englishman and asks for some spare change.

The Englishman says "Neither a borrower nor a lender be. Shakespeare."

The Irishman man says, "Fuck you. Brendan Behan"

Murphy lay in hospital covered in bandages head to foot - with just two little slits for his eyes. 'What happened to you?' asked Cassidy.

'I staggered out of the pub and a lorry hit me a glancing blow and knocked me through a plate glass window.'

'Begod,' said Cassidy. 'It's a good job you were wearing those bandages or you'd have been cut to ribbons!'

Joey-Jim was tooling along the road one fine day when the local policeman, a friend of his, pulled him over. "What's wrong, Seamus?" Joey-Jim asked. "Well didn't ya know, Joey-Jim, that your wife fell out of the car about five miles back?" said Seamus. "Ah, praise the Almighty!" he replied with relief. "I thought I'd gone deaf

Old Scotland. Two nearby castles are at war. One shoots a cannonball at the other. Bang. A piece of wall breaks. In a while the second castle shoots at the first one. A part of a tower becomes a pile of stones. And so on for some time. Then there is a long silence. Suddenly from one of the castles a cry is heard: "Why don't you shoot?" And the answer: "You have the cannonball."

An American tourist was driving in County Kerry, when his motor stopped. He got out to see if he could locate the trouble. A voice behind him said, "The trouble is the carburetor."

He turned around and only saw an old horse. The horse said again, "It's the carburetor that's not working."

The American nearly died with fright, and dashed into the nearest pub, had a large whiskey, and told Murphy the bartender what the horse had said to him.

Murphy said, "Well, don't pay any attention to him, he knows nothing about cars anyway."

Murphy was driving limo in New York and one day he picks up the Pope at Kennedy airport. The Pope tells the Murphy "I like these big cars...you mind if I drive?" So Murphy jumps in the back seat and lets the Pope drive into the city. He gets pulled over by Sullivan the cop who radios his captain and says "I just pulled over a really important guy."

Captain says, "Who is it? Mayor Bloomberg?"

Sullivan says, "Bigger than that. He's got the Pope driving for him."

Mick met Paddy in the street and said, 'Paddy, will you draw your bedroom curtains before making love to your wife in future?'
'Bejaysus Why?' Paddy asked.
'Because,' said Mick, 'The whole street was laughing when they saw you
and your missus making love yesterday.'
Paddy said, 'Stupid bastards, the laugh's on them ...
I wasn't home yesterday.'

Donavan, while visiting Italy, met a sailor from Venice. Before long they found themselves in a tavern. After several hours of heavy drinking the Italian finally slid under the table. The Irishman staggered to his feet and announced, "I'm the first guy who ever drank a Venetian blind!"

Two attorneys went into a diner and ordered two drinks. Then
they produced sandwiches from their briefcases and started to
eat. The owner became quite concerned and marched over and

told them, "You can't eat your own sandwiches in here!"
The attorneys looked at each other, shrugged their shoulders
and then exchanged sandwiches.

Scorcher Murphy was selling his house, and put the matter in an agent's hands. The agent wrote up a sales blurb for the house that made wonderful reading. After Murphy read it, he turned to the agent and asked,"Have I got all ye say there?"The agent said, "Certainly ye have...Why d'ye ask?"Replied Murphy, "Cancel the sale...'tis too good to part with."

Walking into the bar, Mike said to Charlie the bartender, 'Pour me a stiff one - just had another fight with the little woman.'
'Oh yeah?' said Charlie, 'And how did this one end?'
'When it was over,' Mike replied, 'She came to me on her hands and knees.'
'Really,' said Charles, 'Now that's a switch! What did she say?'
She said, 'Come out from under the bed, you little chicken.'

Paddy was driving down the street in a sweat because he had an important meeting and couldn't find a parking place. Looking up to heaven he said, 'Lord take pity on me. If you find me a parking place I will go to Mass every Sunday for the rest of me life and give up me Irish Whiskey!'
Miraculously, a parking place appeared.
Paddy looked up again and said, 'Never mind, I found one.'

An Irish priest is driving down to New York and gets stopped for speeding in Connecticut . The state trooper smells alcohol on the priest's breath and then sees an empty wine bottle on the floor of the car.
He says, 'Sir, have you been drinking?'
'Just water,' says the priest.
The trooper says, 'Then why do I smell wine?'
The priest looks at the bottle and says, 'Good Lord! He's done it again!'

 An Irishman and an Englishman are hunting out in the woods when the Englishman falls to the ground. He doesn't seem to be breathing, his eyes are rolled back in his head. The Irishman whips out his phone and calls the emergency services. He gasps to the operator: "My friend is dead! What can I do?" The operator, in a calm soothing voice says: "Just take it easy. I can help. First, let's make sure he's dead." There is a silence, then a shot is heard. The man's voice comes back on the line. He says: "OK, now what?"

A pompous priest was seated next to an Irishman on a flight home.After the plane was airborne, drink orders were taken. The Irishman asked for an Irish whiskey. The attendant placed the drink on his tray and then asked the priest if he would like a drink. He replied in disgust," I'd rather be savagely ravaged by brazen hussies than let alcohol touch my lips."The Irishman then handed his drink back to the attendant and said "Metoo. I didn't know we had a choice!"

An English builder is keen to implement the EU's policy of job mobility, so he advertises a job in an international trade paper. Three applicants turn up: a Frenchman, a German and an Irishman. When the builder interviews them he points out that a basic knowledge of English is essential, especially of terms used in the building trade, so he has devised a little test. He asks each one of them the same question: " Can you explain to me the difference between 'girder' and 'joist'?"

The Frenchman shrugs his shoulders, admitting that he does not understand the terms. The German also admits that he has no idea.

Before the builder puts the question to the Irishman, he says "I know you speak English, but in the interests of equal treatment I have to ask you the same question as the other two: "What is the difference between 'girder' and 'joist'?"

The Irishman replies, "Sure, everyone knows that. Goethe wrote 'Faust' and Joyce wrote 'Ulysses'."

A 54 year old Irish women woman had a heart attack and was taken to the hospital in Dublin. While on the operating table she had a near death experience.

Seeing God she asked "Is my time up?"

God said, "No, you have another 43 years, 2 months and 8 days to live."

Upon recovery, the woman decided to stay in the hospital and have a face-lift, liposuction, breast implants and a tummy tuck. She even had someone come in and change her hair color and brighten her teeth!

Since she had so much more time to live, she figured she might as well make the most of it. After her last operation, she was released from the hospital.

While crossing the street on her way home, she was killed by an ambulance..

Arriving in front of God, she demanded, "I thought you said I had another 43 years. Why didn't you pull me from out of the path of the ambulance?"

God replied:

"I didn't recognize you!"

An Irishman, is stumbling through the woods, totally drunk, when he comes upon a preacher baptising people in the river.

He proceeds to walk into the water and subsequently bumps into the preacher.

The preacher turns around and is almost overcome by the smell of alcohol, whereupon he asks the drunk,

'Are you ready to find Jesus?'

The drunk shouts, 'Yes, oi am.'

So the preacher grabs him and dunks him in the water.

He pulls him up and asks the drunk, 'Brother have you found Jesus?'

The drunk replies, 'No, oi haven't found Jesus.'

The preacher shocked at the answer, dunks him into the water again for a little longer.

He again pulls him out of the water and asks again, 'Have you found Jesus me brother?'

The drunk again answers, 'No,oi I haven't found Jesus.'

By this time the preacher is at his wits end and
dunks the drunk in the water again —
but this time holds him down for about 30 seconds
and when he begins kicking his arms and legs he
pulls him up.
The preacher again asks the drunk, 'For the love of
God have you found Jesus yet.?'
The Drunk wipes his eyes and catches his breath
and says to the preacher 'Are ya sure dis is where
he fell in?'

Shamus and Murphy fancied a pint or two but
didn't have a lot of money between them, they
could only raise the staggering sum of one Euro.
Murphy said "Hang on, I have an idea."
He went next door to the butcher's shop and came
out with one large sausage.
Shamus said "Are you crazy? Now we don't have
any money left at all!"
Murphy replied, "Don't worry - just follow me."
He went into the pub where he immediately
ordered two pints of Guinness and two glasses of
Jamieson Whisky.
Shamus said "Now you've lost it. Do you know how
much trouble we will be in? We haven't got any
money!!"
Murphy replied, with a smile. "Don't worry, I have
a plan, Cheers!"

They downed their Drinks. Murphy said, "OK, I'll stick the sausage through my zipper and you go on your knees and put it in your mouth."
The barman noticed them, went berserk, and threw them out.
They continued this, pub after pub, getting more and more drunk, all for free..
At the tenth pub Shamus said "Murphy - I don't think I can do any more of this. I'm drunk and me knees are killin' me!"
Murphy said, "How do you think I feel? I lost the sausage in the third pub".

Three Irishman are drinking at a bar. he first says: "Aye, this is a nice bar, but where I come from, there's a better one. At MacDougal's, you buy a drink, you buy another drink, and MacDougal himself will buy your third drink!"
The second then starts: "That sounds like a nice bar, but where I come from, there's a better one called Quinns. At Quinns, you buy a drink, Quinn buys you a drink. You buy another drink, Quinn buys you another drink."
Then the third pipes up. "You think that's good? Where I come from, there's this place called Murphy's. At Murphy's, they buy you your first drink, they buy you your second drink, they buy you your third drink, and then, they take you in the back and get you laid!"

"Wow!" say the other two. "That sounds fantastic! Did that actually happen to you?" "No," replies their friend, "but it happened to my sister!"

Three Irishman are drinking at a bar. he first says: "Aye, this is a nice bar, but where I come from, there's a better one. At MacDougal's, you buy a drink, you buy another drink, and MacDougal himself will buy your third drink!"
The second then starts: "That sounds like a nice bar, but where I come from, there's a better one called Quinns. At Quinns, you buy a drink, Quinn buys you a drink. You buy another drink, Quinn buys you another drink."
Then the third pipes up. "You think that's good? Where I come from, there's this place called Murphy's. At Murphy's, they buy you your first drink, they buy you your second drink, they buy you your third drink, and then, they take you in the back and get you laid!"
"Wow!" say the other two. "That sounds fantastic! Did that actually happen to you?" "No," replies their friend, "but it happened to my sister!"

A passerby watched two Kerry men in a park. One was digging holes and the other was immediately filling them in again. "Tell me," said the passerby,

"What on earth are you doing?" "Well," said the digger,"Usually there are three of us. I dig, Paddy plants the tree and Mick fills in the hole. Today Paddy is off ill, but that doesn't mean Mick and I get the day off, does it?"

Seamus O'Brien had been hailed as the most intelligent Irish man for three years running. He had topped such shows as Larry Gogans 'Just a Minute Quiz' and 'Quicksilver'. It was suggested by the Irish Mensa board that he should enter into the English Mastermind Championships. He did, and won a place. On the evening of the competition, Seamus walks on stage, sits down and makes himself comfortable. The lights dim and a spotlight shines on his face. Magnus, the emcee, proceeds: "Seamus, what subject are you studying?" Seamus responds, "Irish history". "Very well," says Magnus, "your first question - in what year did the 'Easter Rising take place?" "Pass," says Seamus. "Okay," says Magnus, "Who was the leader of the Easter Rising?" Seamus responds,"Pass." "Well then," says Magnus, "how long did the Easter Rising last?" Again, Seamus responds, "Pass." Instantly, a voice from the audience shouts out: "Good man, Seamus - tell the English nothing..."

A dietitian was addressing a large audience in Dublin. "The material we put into our stomachs is enough to have killed most of us sitting here, years ago. Red meat is awful. Soft drinks erode your stomach lining. Chinese food is loaded with MSG. Vegetables can be disastrous, and none of us realizes the long-term harm caused by the germs in our drinking water. But there is one food that is the most dangerous of all and we all have, or will, eat it. Can anyone here tell me what food it is that causes the most grief and suffering for years after eating it?"

A mother was preparing pancakes for her sons, Kevin, 5, and Ryan, 3. The boys began to squabble over who would get the first pancake. Their mother saw the opportunity for a moral lesson. "If Jesus were sitting here, He would say, 'Let my brother have the first pancake, I can wait.'" Kevin turned to his younger brother and said, "Ryan, you be Jesus!"

Paddy was in New York. He was patiently waiting and watching the traffic cop on a busy street crossing. The cop stopped the flow of traffic and shouted, 'Okay, pedestrians.' Then he'd allow the traffic to pass. He'd done this several times, and Paddy still stood on the sidewalk. After the cop had shouted, 'Pedestrians!' for the tenth time, Paddy went over to him and said, 'Is it not about time ye let the Catholics across?'

Gallagher opened the morning newspaper and was dumbfounded to read in the obituary column that he had died. He quickly phoned his best friend, Finney.

'Did you see the paper?' asked Gallagher. 'They say I died!!'

'Yes, I saw it!' replied Finney. 'Where are ye callin' from?'

Father Murphy walks into a pub in Donegal, and asks the first man he meets, 'Do you want to go to heaven?'

The man said, 'I do, Father.'

The priest said, 'Then stand over there against the wall.'

Then the priest asked the second man, 'Do you want to go to heaven?'

'Certainly, Father,' the man replied.

'Then stand over there against the wall,' said the priest.

Then Father Murphy walked up to O'Toole and asked, 'Do you want to go to heaven?'

O'Toole said, 'No, I don't Father.'

The priest said, 'I don't believe this. You mean to tell me that when you die you don't want to go to heaven?'

O'Toole said, 'Oh, when I die , yes. I thought you were getting a group together to go right now.'

A minister was completing a temperance sermon. With great emphasis he said, "If I had all the beer in the world, I'd take it and pour it into the river." With even greater emphasis he said, "And if I had all the wine in the world, I'd take it and pour it into the river." And then finally, shaking his fist in the air, he said, "And if I had all the whiskey in the world,I'd take it and pour it into the river." Sermon complete, he then sat down. The choir director stood very cautiously and announced with a smile, for our closing selection,let us sing Hymn #365, "Shall We Gather at the River."

An attractive young lady was on a plane arriving from Ireland. She found herself seated next to an elderly priest whom she asked: "Excuse me Father, could I ask a favor?" "Of course my child, What can I do for you?" "Here is the problem.I bought myself a new sophisticated vibrating hair remover for which I paid an enormous sum of money. I have really gone over the declaration limits and I am worried that they will confiscate it at customs. Do you think you could hide it under your cassock?" "Of course I could, my child, but you must realize that I cannot lie." "You have such an honest face Father, I am sure they will not ask you any questions", and she gave him the worrisome personal gadget. The aircraft arrived at its destination. When the priest presented himself to customs he was asked, "Father, do you have anything to declare?" "From the top of my head to my sash, I have nothing to declare, my son", he replied. Finding his reply strange, the customs officer asked, "And from the sash down, what do you have?" The priest replied, "I have there a marvelous little instrument destined for use by women, but which has never been used." Breaking out in laughter, the customs officer said, "Go ahead Father. Next!"

A minister dies and is waiting in line at the Pearly Gates. Ahead of him is a lad dressed in sunglasses, loud shirt, leather jacket, and jeans. Saint Peter addresses the lad: "Who are you, so that I may know whether or not to admit you to the Kingdom of Heaven?" The fellah replies, "I'm Johnny O'Rourke, taxi-driver, Brooklyn, New York." Saint Peter consults his list. He smiles and says to the taxi-driver, "Take this silken robe and golden staff and enter the Kingdom of Heaven." The taxi-driver goes into Heaven with his robe and staff, and it's the minister's turn. He stands erect and booms out,

"I am Phillip Smith, pastor of Saint Mary's for the last forty-three years." Saint Peter consults his list. He says to the minister, "Take this cotton robe and wooden staff and enter the Kingdom of Heaven." "Just a minute," says the minister. "That man was a taxi-driver and he gets a silken robe and golden staff. How can this be?" "Up here, we work by results," says Saint Peter. "While you preached, people slept; while he drove, people prayed."

A Jesuit priest decided to visit a small island off the coast of Connemara. The inhabitants numbered no more than a couple of dozen, but the priest threw himself into the Lord's work with a vengeance. Having taken over the bar of the pub for Mass, and having delivered a fire and brimstone sermon, he questioned his small congregation. "How long is it since any of you had your confessions heard?" he asked. "Well, Father,' answered Brendan, the oldest inhabitant. "It must be three years since the last priest was here." "Why didn't you make a trip to the mainland?" thundered the priest. "Well, Father,' said Brendan, "the water between us and the mainland is very rough, and our boat is old and leaky. So you see. if we've only venial sins to confess, it's not worth the bother, and if we've mortal sins, it's not worth the risk!"

Sean got home in the early hours of the morning after a night at the local pub. He made such a racket as he weaved his way through the house that he woke up the wife."By all the saints, what are you doing down there?"she shouted from the bedroom. "Get yourself up here and don't be waking the neighbours." "I'm trying to get a barrel of Guinness up the stairs," he shouted back. "Leave it 'till the morning," she shouted down. "I can't" says he, "I've drank it!"

A couple had two little boys, ages 8 and 10, who were excessively mischievous. They were always getting into trouble and their parents knew that, if any mischief occurred in their village, their sons were probably involved. The boys' mother heard that the local vicar had been successful in disciplining children, so she asked if he would speak with her boys. The vicar agreed, but asked to see them individually. So the mother sent her 8-year-old in first that morning; with the older boy to see the vicar in the afternoon. The vicar, a huge man with a booming voice, sat the younger boy down and asked him sternly, "Where is God?" The boy's mouth dropped open, but he made no response, sitting there with his mouth hanging open, wide eyed. So the vicar repeated the question in an even sterner tone, "Where is God!!?" Again the boy made no attempt to answer. So the vicar raised his voice even more and shook his finger in the boy's face and bellowed, "WHERE IS GOD!!!!?" The boy screamed and bolted from the room, ran directly home and dived into a cupboard, slamming the door behind him. When his older brother found him in the cupboard , he asked, "What happened?" The younger brother, gasping for breath, replied, "We are in BIG trouble this time. God is missing - and they think WE did it.!"

Sally was driving home from one of her business trips in Northern Ireland when she saw an elderly woman walking on the side of the road. As the trip was a long and quiet one, she stopped the car and asked the woman if she would like a ride. After a bit of small talk and while resuming the journey the woman noticed a brown bag on the seat next to Sally. What's in the bag?" asked the woman. Sally looked down at the brown bag and said, "It's a bottle of wine, I got it for my husband." The woman was silent for a moment. Then speaking with the quiet wisdom of an elder she said: "Good trade."

For many years Kate Murphy had run the fruit and vegetable stall in the town market and she'd learned to have an answer for any situation. So there she stood, watching the big Texan who was poking around the stall. 'Hey, what are these?' he asked. 'Apples,' said Kate. 'Apples?' laughed the Yank. 'Why, in Texas we have apples twice that size! And what are these?' "Those are potatoes,' said Kate. 'Potatoes? Where I come from, bragged the Texan, our potatoes are twice as big at least,' Just then he picked up a cabbage, but before he could speak Kate said: 'If you're not buying Brussels sprouts, you'd best be putting that down.'

When my wife's sister, Patty, was very young, she was allowed to have her best friend, a boy named Rory, over to spend the night. As the children grew toward adolescence, their parents knew that someday the sleepovers would have to end. One night, when Rory and his family were visiting, everyone gathered around the television to watch the Rose of Tralee pageant. When Patty asked if Rory could stay over, the parents hesitated, wondering if the time had finally come to discontinue the tradition. At that moment, the pageant host announced a contestant's measurements: 36-22-36. "Rory," his mother asked, "what are those numbers?" The boy thought for only a moment before responding, "Ninety-four?"

Rory was allowed to stay.

Two Irish women walking through the forest one day hear a voice coming from near a log."Help me." They lifted the log and underneath found a frog. "Help me " said the frog "I am an investment banker turned into a frog by an evil curse. I need to be kissed by a woman and I will turn back into an investment banker." One of the women grabbed the frog and stuffed it into her handbag. Aghast, her friend said, "Did you not hear the frog? He needs to to be returned to being an investment banker." "Listen", her friend said."these days a talking frog is worth a lot more than an investment banker."

The teacher asked each of her students how they celebrated Christmas. She calls first on young Patrick O'Flaherty. "Tell me, Patrick, what do you do at Christmas time? Patrick addresses the class: "Me and my twelve brothers and sisters go to midnight Mass and we sing carols. Then we come home very late and we hang up our pillowcases at the foot of the bed. Then we go to bed and wait for Father Christmas to come with all our toys." "Very nice, Patrick," the teacher says. "Now, Billy Murphy, what do you do at Christmas?" "Me and my sister go to church with Mum and Dad, and we also sing carols. When we get home, we put biscuits and milk by the chimney and hang up our stockings. We hardly sleep waiting for Santa Claus to bring our presents." "That's also very nice, Billy," she said. Realizing that there was a Jewish boy in the class and not wanting to leave him out of the discussion, she asked him the same question. "Now, Isaac, what do you do at Christmas?" "Well, we also sing carols," Isaac responds. Surprised, the teacher questions further. "Tell us what you sing." "Well, it's the same thing every year. Dad comes home from the office. We all pile into the Rolls Royce and drive to his toy factory. When we get inside, we look at all the empty shelves and sing, 'What a friend we have in Jesus.' Then we all go to the Bahamas."

A Man wakes up in the morning, sees a gorilla in the tree outside his window.

Calls up the zoo. "I got your gorilla in the tree outside my window."

Zoo says, "Okay, we'll send a man right over."

Man says, "Waitaminit! Waitaminit! That's a big gorilla! It's gonna take more than one man to get it outta the tree!"

Comes a knock on the door. It's five foot Murphy from the zoo. Murphy says, "Okay,Boy-ho. Here's our plan."

Man says, "Waitaminit! Waitaminit! What do you mean--our plan? That's your gorilla, you get it out of the tree."

Little Murphy from the zoo says, "Don't worry, Boy-ho. You got the easy part. You stay on the ground. I got the hard part. I climb up in the tree. Okay. I got a shotgun, a broom handle, a savage Dalmatian dog, and a pair of handcuffs. I climb up in the tree, I push the gorilla out with the broom handle. The gorilla hits the ground. The dog runs over and bites the gorilla on the balls. The gorilla screams and throws his hands up in the air. You run over, slap on the cuffs, and I take him back to the zoo."

"Waitaminit! Waitaminit!" the man says. "What's the shotgun for?"

"Listen, Boy-ho. If I fall out of the tree instead of that gorilla, shoot the dog!"

A policeman pulls over a speeding car. He says, "I clocked you at 80 miles per hour, sir." The driver says, "Are you sure? I had it on cruise control at 60, perhaps your radar gun needs calibrating."

Not looking up from her knitting the wife says: "Now don't be silly dear, you know that this car doesn't have cruise control."

As the cop writes out the ticket, the driver looks over at his wife and growls, "Can't you please keep your mouth shut for once?"

As the cops makes out the second ticket for the illegal use of a radar detector unit, the man glowers at his wife and says through clenched teeth,

"Woman ,didn't I tell you to keep your mouth shut!"

The cops frowns and says "And I notice that you're not wearing your seat belt, sir. That's an on the spot 60 euro fine."

The driver says, "Well, you see sir, I had it on, but took it off when you pulled me over so that I could get my license out of my back pocket."

The wife says, "Now, dear, you know very well that you didn't have your seat belt on. You never wear your seat belt when you're driving."

And as the cop is writing out the third ticket the driver turns to his wife and barks, "WHY DON'T YOU PLEASE SHUT UP?"

The cop looks over at the woman and asks, "Does your husband always talk to you this way, Ma'am?"

Smiling sweetly, she replies. Only when he's been drinking, sir."

The store manager, O'Reilly, heard Maryann his assistant tell a customer, "No mam, we haven't had any for a while, and it doesn't look as if we'll be getting any soon." O'Reilly was horrified and ran over to the customer and said, "Of course we'll have some soon. We placed an order last week." Then he took the assistant aside and said, "Never, never, say we're out of anything - say we've got it on order and it's coming. Now what was it she wanted?" "Rain," said the assistant.

An Irishman, a Mexican and a blond guy were doing construction work on the roof of a skyscraper. They were eating lunch and the Irishman said, "Corned beef and cabbage. If I get corned beef and cabbage one more time for lunch I'm going to jump off this building." The Mexican opened his lunch box and exclaimed, "Burritos again! If I get burritos one more time I'm going to jump off, too." The blond opened his lunch and said, "Bologna again. If I get a bologna sandwich one more time, I'm jumping as well." The next day the Irishman opened his lunch box, saw corned beef and cabbage and jumped. The Mexican opened his lunch, saw a burrito and jumped. The blond guy opened his lunch, saw the bologna and jumped. At the funeral, the Irishman's wife was weeping. She said, "If I'd known how tired he was of corned beef and cabbage, I never would have given it to him again!" The Mexican's wife also wept and said, "I could have given him tacos or enchiladas! I didn't realize he was so bored with burritos." Everyone turned and stared at the blonde guy's wife...
wait for it.........
Hey, don't look at me," she said, "He makes his own lunch."

Three priests went for a ramble in the country. It was unusually hot for Ireland in September and before too long, they were sweating profusely. They came upon a small lake and since it was fairly secluded, they took off all their clothes and jumped into the water. Feeling refreshed, the trio decided to pick a few blackberries while enjoying their "freedom". As they were crossing an open area, they saw a group of ladies from the village coming towards them. Unable to get to their clothes in time, two of the priests covered their privates, but the third one covered his face while they ran for cover. After the ladies had left and the men got their clothes back on, the first two priests asked the third why he covered his face rather than his privates. "I don't know about you two," he replied, "but in my parish, it's my face they would recognize."

Two Irish men are in a plane. The roof comes off! Mick says to Paddy, "If this plane turns upside down will we fall out??"
"No way Mick" says Paddy, "we'll still be best friends."

A Catholic priest, a Protestant minister, and a Jewish rabbi were discussing when life begins. "Life begins," said the priest, "at the moment of fertilization. That is when God instills the spark of life into the fetus." "We believe," said the minister, "that life begins at birth, because that is when the baby becomes an individual and is capable of making its own decisions and must learn about sin." "You're both wrong," said the rabbi. "Life begins when the children have graduated and moved out of the house."

Father Doyle was a clever speaker and a firm advocate of abstinence, the closure of pubs on Sundays, and a standard of morality that would ensure a warm welcome in Heaven. One Sunday morning, among his listeners was a young country girl who was new to the parish. She was deeply impressed with the priest's eloquent preaching. Indeed, so impressed that she included a few lines about him in her next letter home:
"I never get tired of listening to Father Doyle. He is such a lovely speaker, you'd swear that every word he says is true."

In Killarney, an American tourist sees a sign in front of a farmhouse: "Talking Dog for Sale." He rings the bell and the farmer tells him the dog is around the back. The tourist goes behind the house and sees a black mutt just sitting there "You talk?" he asks. "Indeed." the dog replies. "So, what's your story?" The mutt looks up and says, "Well, I discovered my gift of talking when I was very young and I wanted to be of help to humanity, so I told Interpol about my gift; in no time they had me flying from country to country, sitting in rooms with world leaders, because no one would believe a dog would be listening. I was one of their most valuable spies for eight years running. The jetting around really tired me out, and I knew I wasn't getting any younger. So I signed up for a job at the airport to do some undercover security work, mostly wandering near suspicious characters and eavesdropping. I uncovered some very shady dealings there and was awarded a ton of medals. Then I settled down, had a wife, a dozen or so puppies, and now I'm just retired." The tourist is amazed. He goes back and asks the farmer what he wants for the dog. The farmer says, "Ten euros, sir." The tourist sputters, "But that dog is incredible. Why on earth are you selling him so cheap?" The farmer shrugs and says "Ah well, sir, you, see, isn't he just the biggest liar this side of Croagh Patrick? He's done none of what he told ye."

The concierge at a posh resort was often asked about the ski facilities. One day a couple who had just checked in after a long flight came by and asked me where the lift was. "Go down the hill," he told them, "out the door, past the pool, 200 yards down the block, and you'll see it on your right." Their tired faces suddenly looked even more exhausted until the man behind them spoke up. "They're from Ireland," he said. "I think they're looking for the elevator."

Katie and Moira are old friends. They have both been married to their husbands for a long time. Katie is upset because she thinks her husband doesn't find her attractive anymore. "As I get older he doesn't bother to look at me!" she complains to Moira. "What a pity," says Moira. As I get older my husband says I get more beautiful every day. "All well and good, says Katie, but your husband's an antique dealer!"

A man and his wife, now in their 60's, were celebrating their 40th wedding anniversary. On their special day, a good fairy came to them and said that because they had been such a devoted couple she would grant each of them a very special wish. The wife wished for a trip around the world with her husband. Whoosh! Immediately she had airline & cruise tickets in her hands. The man wished for a female companion, 30 years younger..... Whoosh! Immediately he turned ninety!!!

At every tea-break, Sean, the hod-carrier was always boasting to his older work-mate, Mike the brick- layer, that he was the better worker because he was stronger, faster, and younger. Mike stoically put up with the bragging until one day, he couldn't take it any more. "Well, Sean", he said, I'll bet a week's wages I can haul something in a wheelbarrow over to that building that you won't be able to wheel back." Sean laughed derisively and agreed to the bet. With that, Mike grabbed the handles of the wheelbarrow and told Sean to get in.

A wealthy couple from Texas were touring Ireland and found themselves in a tiny rural village at lunchtime. The only place serving food was a somewhat rustic looking cafe which in their opinion, had seen better days. Having no other choice, they carefully stepped over the pooch snoozing on the threshold and went inside. As they sat down, the husband frowned as he brushed some crumbs from his chair and his wife did likewise as she wiped the table with her napkin.The waitress came over and asked if they would like to see a menu. "No thanks," said the husband. "I'll just have a cup of tea with cream and sugar."I'll have the same", his wife said. "And please make sure the cup is clean." Unphased by the rudeness of the remark, the waitress smiled and marched off into the kitchen. A few minutes later, she was back."Two cups of tea," she announced in her lovely lilting Irish brogue..."And which one of you was it who wanted the clean cup?"

Charlie was a regular visitor at the Galway Races. One afternoon he noticed an unusual sight. Right before the first race, a Catholic priest visited one of the horses in the stable area and gave it a blessing. Charlie watched the race very carefully, and sure enough the blessed horse came in first! Charlie followed the priest before the next race, and again he went to the stables and performed a similar procedure. Thinking there might be something to it, Charlie put a couple of euros on the blessed horse. Sure enough it came in by two lengths and Charlie won close to fifty euros! The priest continued the same procedure through the next few races and Charlie won each time. He was now ahead a thousand, so between races Charlie left the track, went to the bank and withdrew his life's savings. The biggest race of the day was the last one. Charlie followed the priest and watched which horse he blessed. He then went to the betting window and put every euro he owned on that horse to win. The race began. Down the stretch they came, and as they crossed the finish line, Charlie's pick was last! Devastated, he found the priest and told him that he had been watching him bless the horses all day, and they all became winners except the last horse on which he had bet his life savings. Charlie then asked, "What happened to the last horse which you blessed? Why didn't it win like the others?" "Ye must be a Protestant," sighed the priest. "The trouble is you can't tell the difference between a blessing and the last rites."

"Which is the first and most important sacrament?" asked the Catechism teacher. "Marriage", avowed Moira. "No, baptism is the first and most important sacrament," corrected the teacher. "Not in our family," retorted Moira, in a haughty voice. "We're decent people!"

An elderly woman died last month. Having never married, she requested no male pallbearers. In her handwritten instructions for her memorial service, she wrote, "They wouldn't take me out while I was alive, I don't want them to take me out when I'm dead."

Attending a wedding for the first time, a little girl whispered to her mother, "Why is the lady all dressed in white?" "Because white is the color of happiness, and today is the happiest day of her life. The child thought about this for a moment, then said, "So why is the man wearing black?"

A man was brought to Mercy Hospital, and taken quickly in for coronary surgery. The operation went well and, as the groggy man regained consciousness, he was reassured by a Sister of Mercy, who was waiting by his bed. "Mr. O'Toole, you're going to be just fine," said the nun, gently patting his hand. "We do need to know, however, how you intend to pay for your stay here. Are you covered by insurance?" "No, sorry, I don't have any insurance," the man whispered hoarsely. "Can you pay in cash?" asked the nun. "I'm afraid I cannot, Sister." "Well, do you have any close relatives?" the nun persisted. "Just my sister in America" he volunteered. "But she's a humble spinster nun." "Oh, I must correct you, Mr. O'Toole. Nuns are not 'spinsters;' they are married to God." "Wonderful," said O'Toole. "In that case, please send the bill to my brother-in-law."

Father Murphy went out one Saturday to visit his parishioners. At one house it was obvious that someone was home, but nobody came to the door even though the priest had knocked several times. Finally, he took out his card and wrote "Revelations 3:20" on the back of it, and stuck it in the door: "Behold, I stand at the door and knock. If anyone hears my voice and opens the door, I will come in to him and dine with him and him with me." The next day, the card turned up in the collection plate. Below Father Murphy's message was the notation "Genesis 3:10": "I heard your voice in the garden and I was afraid because I was naked; and I hid myself."

Q: How many Irishmen does it take to change a light bulb?
A: Three. One to hold the bulb, one to screw it in, and one to say how grand the old one was.

An Irish lady goes to the bar on a cruise ship and orders a Jameson with two drops of water. As the bartender gives her the drink she says, "I'm on this cruise to celebrate my 80th birthday and it's today." The bartender says, "Well, since it's your birthday, I'll buy you a drink. In fact, this one is on me." "Well, thank you kindly, sir" says she. As the woman finishes her drink, the woman to her right says, "I would like to buy you a drink, too." The old woman says, "Thank you. Bartender, I'll have a Jameson with two drops of water." "Coming up," says the bartender. As she finishes that drink, the man to her left says, "I would like to buy you one, too." The old woman says, "Thank you. Bartender, I'll have another Jameson with two drops of water." "Coming right up," the bartender says. As he gives her the drink, he says, "Ma'am, I'm dying of curiosity. Why the Jameson with only two drops of water?" The old woman replies, "Ah, lad, when you're my age, you've learned how to hold the hard stuff. Holding your water, however, is another matter entirely."

❦

While working on a lesson in world religions, a kindergarten teacher asked her students to bring something related to their family's faith to class. At the appropriate time, she asked the students to come forward and share with the rest of the students. The first child said, "I am Muslim, and this is my prayer rug."
The second child said, "I am Jewish, and this is my Star of David."
The third child said, "I am Catholic, and this is my rosary."
The final child said, "I am Protestant, and this is my casserole dish.

Pat and Mike are drinking in the done-up version of their local pub, The Continental Bistro and Bar in the Ballybegorrah Arms Hotel, Killarney. They take in the no-sawdust on the new Italian tile floor; the hi-back red leather bar stools; the bowls of free black olives, cashew nuts and tasty "tapas" on the shiny, black, two inch thick, granite counter. "Ye know", Pat," says Mike, "it's all brilliant, but I miss the auld spittoon." Pat takes his pipe from his mouth, sips his pint, then says,"You always did, me auld friend. You always did."

Mrs. Pete Monaghan came into the newsroom to pay for her husband's obituary. She was told by the kindly newsman that it was dollar a word and he remembered Pete and wasn't it too bad about him passing away. She thanked him for his kind words and bemoaned the fact that she only had two dollars. But she wrote out the obituary, "Pete died." The newsman said he thought old Pete deserved more and he'd give her three more words at no charge. Mrs. Pete Monaghan thanked him and rewrote the obituary: "Pete died. Boat for sale"

Morris walks out into the street and hails a taxi just going by. He gets into the taxi, and the cabbie says, "Perfect timing. You're just like Liam." "Who?" "Liam O'Connor. There's a lad who did everything right. Like my coming along when you needed a cab. It would have happened like that to Liam.""Every path has its puddle" says Morris."

"It wasn't like that with Liam," says the cabbie."He was a brilliant athlete. He could have played football for Kerry. He could golf with the pros. He sang like Ronan Tynon and he danced like Michael Flatley. What's more, he had a memory like Methusalah. He could remember everyone's birthday. He knew all about wine, which fork to eat with. He could fix anything. Not like me. I change a fuse, and the whole town goes out."

"No wonder you remember him." says Morris. "Well, I never actually met the man." "Then how do you know so much about him?" asks Morris. "I married his widow."

A young lad had just gotten his provisional license. (learner's permit) He asked his father, who was a minister, if they could discuss his use of the car. His father said to him, "If you bring your marks up, study your bible, and get your hair cut, we'll talk about it." A month later the boy came back and again asked his father if they could now discuss his use of the car. His father said, "Well, son, I see that

your marks have improved, you've studied your
bible diligently, but you didn't get a hair cut!" The
young man waited a moment and then replied,
"You know dad, I've been thinking about that.
Didn't Samson have long hair, Moses have long
hair, Noah have long hair, and even Jesus himself
have long hair?" His father replied, "They did so,
and they walked everywhere they went!"

Two lovely old biddies had been friends for many
decades. Over the years they had shared all kinds of
activities and adventures. Lately, their activities
had been limited to meeting a few times a week for
a cup of tea and a natter. One day they were sipping
their tea when one looked at the other and said,
"Now don't go getting upset with me...I know we've
been pals for a long time.....but I just can't think of
your name! I've thought and thought, but I can't
remember it. Please tell me what your name is. Her
friend glared at her. For at least three minutes she
just stared and glared. At last, she said, "How soon
do you need to know?

Twins Jack and Sarah were always squabbling.
Tired of listening to them yelling at each other and
knowing full well neither one would admit they
were in the wrong, their mother says, "I have an

idea: Sarah, why don't you tell Jack you were wrong, and Jack, you tell Sarah she was right. So, Sarah says to Jack "I was wrong." Jack grins and says to Sarah: "You are right."

The man from the window company called Miss O'Leary on the telephone. "Miss O'Leary, he says, you haven't made a single payment on your new windows. Is there something the matter?" Bristling with annoyance, Miss O'Leary replies. "I may be up in years, but I still have my wits about me. Wasn't your man after telling me those windows would pay for themselves in a year?"

A curious fellow died one day and found himself waiting in the long line of judgment. As he stood there he noticed that some souls were allowed to march right through the pearly gates into Heaven. Others though, were led over to Satan who threw them into the burning pit. But every so often, instead of hurling a poor soul into the fire, Satan would toss a soul off to one side into a small pile. After watching Satan do this several times, the fellow's curiosity got the best of him. So he strolled over and asked Satan what he was doing. "Excuse me, Prince of Darkness," he said. "I'm waiting in line for judgment, but I couldn't help wondering, why are you tossing those people aside instead of flinging them into the Fires of Hell with the others?" "Ah, those ...Satan said with a groan. "They're all from Ireland. They're still too cold and damp to burn."

Three men were sitting together bragging about how they had set their new wives straight on their domestic duties. The first man had married a woman from Italy and boasted that he had told his wife she was to do all the dishes and house cleaning that needed to be done. He said that it took a couple days but on the third day he came home to a clean house and the dishes were all washed and put away. The second man had married a woman from France. He bragged that he had given his wife orders that she was to do all the cleaning, all the dishes, and the cooking. He told them that the first day he didn't see any results, but the next day it was better. By the third day, his house was clean, the dishes were done, and he had a delicious dinner on the. table. The third man had married an Irish girl. He boasted that he told her his house was to be cleaned, the dishes washed, the cooking done and the laundry washed. And this was all entirely her responsibility. He said the first day he didn't see anything and the second day he didn't see anything, but by the third day some of the swelling had gone down so he could see a little out of his left eye!

An Irishman died and went to heaven. As he stood in front of St. Peter at the Pearly Gates, he saw a huge wall of clocks behind him. He asked, "What are all those clocks?" St. Peter answered, "Those are Lie-Clocks. Everyone in the universe has a Lie-Clock. Every time you lie, the hands on your clock will move." "Oh," said the man, "whose clock is that?" "That's St. Patrick's. The hands have never moved, indicating that he never told a lie." "Incredible," said the man. "And whose clock is that one?" St. Peter responded, "That's Daniel O'Connell's clock. The hands have moved twice, telling us that he told only two lies in his entire life." "Where's Bertie Ahern's clock?" asked the man. "Bertie's clock is in God's office. He's using it as a ceiling fan."

Two men walked into a pub late one afternoon and noticed that, among the few customers, was one individual sitting quietly at the end of the bar. The two ordered some beers. The bartender brought them and said, "that will be 50p please." They put it on the slate and a short time later ordered two more beers; again they were charged 25p each. The two could not believe the price and after having a third beer for the same amount, they decided to ask the bartender what the catch was. The bartender replied, "there is no catch, gentlemen. I have just started brewing this beer on the premises and I'm selling it below cost to introduce it to my customers. I'm happy to see you're enjoying it." Indeed, they noticed that almost everyone was enjoying the beer and the remarkable price except for the one man at the end of the bar. He had not ordered anything since the two came in. Becoming very curious about this individual, the two asked the bartender, "Doesn't he ever order anything?" "Oh yes," said the bartender. "That's Patrick Curran, our local accountant. He's waiting for happy hour."

A man and a woman, who have never met before, find themselves assigned to the same sleeping room on a transcontinental train. Though initially embarrassed and uneasy over sharing a room, the two are tired and fall asleep quickly - he in the upper bunk and she in the lower. At 2:00AM, he leans over and gently wakes the woman, saying, "Ma'am, I'm sorry to bother you, but would you be willing to reach into the cupboard to get me a second blanket? I'm awfully cold." "I have a better idea," she replies. "Just for tonight, let's pretend that we're married." "That's a great idea!" he exclaims. "Good," she replies. "Get up and get your own blanket."

The spring bank holiday was over and the teacher asked the class how they had spent the time. Kevin eagerly put up his hand. "We visited our cousins in Carrigaline!" "Well, Kevin," says the teacher, "that sounds like a brilliant vocabulary word - can you tell the class how to spell Carrigaline?" Kevin furrowed his brow, chewed on his lip, and then said with a big grin, "Em, well now, come to think of it, we went to Cork!"

A man walked into the lingerie department of Dunnes in Dublin and said to the woman behind the counter, "I'd like to buy a Baptist bra for my wife, size 36B." What type of bra? asked the clerk. "Baptist" said the man. She said get a Baptist bra, and that you'd know what she meant." "Ah yes, now I remember" said the saleslady. "We don't sell many of those. Mostly our customers want the Catholic type, the Salvation Army type. or the Presbyterian type."Confused the man asked, "What's the difference between them?" The lady responded, "It is all really quite simple; the Catholic type supports the masses, the Salvation Army type lifts up the fallen, and the Presbyterian type keeps them staunch and upright. Then there's the Baptist type." "What does that do?" asked the man. She replied, "It makes mountains out of molehills."

While impatiently waiting for a table in a restaurant, Miss O'Leary says to Mrs. Clancy, "If they weren't so crowded in here all the time, they'd do a lot more business."

The first priest says, "You know, since the warm weather started, I've been having trouble with mice in my church. I've tried everything - noise, cats, spray, nothing seems to scare them away." The second priest says, "My church, too. There are hundreds of them living in the cellar. I've set traps and even called in an expert exterminator. Nothing has worked so far." The third priest says, "I had the same problem. So I baptized them all and made them members of my parish. Haven't seen one of them since."

Miss O'Leary, our lovely little old spinster from Leitrim makes a return visit this week. After Mass one Sunday, she went up to the priest and said, "I have to tell you Father, your sermons are a wonder to behold. Sure we didn't know what sin was till you came to the parish!"

A pompous priest was seated next to an Irishman on a flight home. After the plane was airborne, drink orders were taken. The Irishman asked for an Irish whiskey. The attendant placed the drink on his tray and then asked the priest if he would like a drink. He replied in disgust," I'd rather be savagely ravaged by brazen hussies than let alcohol touch my lips." The Irishman then handed his drink back to the attendant and said "Me
 too. I didn't know we had a choice!"

A surgeon and an architect, both English, were joined by an Irish politician, and all fell to arguing as to whose profession was the oldest. Said the surgeon, "Eve was made from Adam's rib, and that surely was a surgical operation." "Maybe," said the architect, "but prior to that, order was created out of chaos, and that was an architectural job." "Sure now," interrupted the politician, "but wasn't somebody after creating the chaos first?"

Sean goes into the pub and asks for three Guinness. He sits there and sips from the first one, then the second, and the third. He does this until finally all three pints are finished. He pays the bill and leaves. A couple of nights later he comes back and repeats the ritual. This goes on for a while and finally the bartender's curiosity gets the better of him and he asks why the three Guinness and why drink them all together the way he does. "Well, " says Sean, "My brother Michael is in the USA and my other brother Liam is in Australia. We can't meet in the pub and share a Guinness, so we have an agreement that whenever we go have a drink, we order three pints and pretend we're together." The bartender thinks to himself, "What a wonderful idea." A few months go by and one night Sean comes in and he orders two Guinness. The bartender is afraid to ask, but Sean seems fine, so finally the bartender says, "I see you've only ordered two Guinness tonight. Did something happen to one of your brothers?"No, no," says Sean, "They're both fit as a fiddle and healthy as horses!" "So why only the two Guinness?" asks the bartender. "Ah, well now," says Sean, "I've given up Guinness for Lent."

Sean is walking through the park and notices an old lady sitting on a bench sobbing her eyes out. He stops and asks her what is wrong. She says, "I have a 22-year old husband at home. He kisses and cuddles me every morning and then gets up and makes me eggs, bacon, black pudding, toast and tea." Well then," Sean says, "Why are you crying?" She says, "He makes me homemade soup for lunch and then kisses and cuddles me for half the afternoon." Perplexed, Sean says, "So, why are you crying?" She says, "For supper, he always makes me my favourite meal and then kisses and cuddles me until 2:00 a.m. Astonished by now, Sean says, "Why in the world would you be crying, then?" Says she, "I can't remember where I live!"

When my older brother was very young, he always walked up to the church altar with my mother when she took communion. On one occasion, he tugged at her arm and asked, "What does the priest say when he gives you the bread?" Mom whispered something in his ear. Imagine his shock many years later when he learned that the priest doesn't say, "Be quiet until you get to your seat."

It's Christmas time and Paddy and Shaun decide to go look for a Christmas Tree. They gather their axe, a sled, and a broom to brush the trees off so they can get a good look at them.
When they finally reach a fine group of trees, Shaun brushes off the first tree, and stands back

with Paddy to look at it. "Well, Paddy, What do you think?"

"Sorry, Shaun, this tree won't do. Let's try another one."

They come upon another nice tree, Shaun brushes it off, and they both look at it. "How about this one, Paddy?"

"Not quite, Shaun. Let's keep looking."

This goes on until nightfall. Both Paddy and Shaun are cold, tired, and hungry. "Well, Paddy, what do we do now?"

"Shaun, I think we should take home the next tree we find, whether it has lights on it or not..."

An Irish daughter had not been home for over 5 years.

Upon her return, her Father cussed her.

"Where have ye been all this time? Why did ye not write to us, not even a line?"

"Why didn't ye call? Can ye not understand what ye put yer old Mother thru?"

The girl, crying, replied, "Sniff, sniff....Dad....I became a prostitute..."

"Ye what!!? Out of here, ye shameless harlot! Sinner! You're a disgrace to this Catholic family."

"OK, Dad-- as ye wish."

"I just came back to give mum this luxurious fur coat, title deed to a ten bedroom mansion plus a $5 million savings certificate."

"For me little brother, this gold Rolex."
"And for ye Daddy, the sparkling new Mercedes limited edition convertible that's parked outside plus a membership to the country club..............
(takes a breath)............. and an invitation for ye all to spend New Year's Eve on board my new yacht in the Riviera and....."
"Now what was it ye said ye had become?" says Dad.
Girl, crying again, "Sniff, sniff....a prostitute Daddy! Sniff, sniff."
"Oh! Be Jesus! Ye scared me half to death, girl!"
"I thought ye said a Protestant, come here and give yer old Dad a hug."

The wise old Mother Superior from county Tipperary was dying. The nuns gathered around her bed trying to make her comfortable. They gave her some warm milk to drink, but she refused it. Then one nun took the glass back to the kitchen. Remembering a bottle of Irish whiskey they had received as a gift the previous Christmas, she opened and poured a generous amount into the warm milk.
When she walked back at Mother Superior's bed, she held the glass to her lips. Mother drank a little, then a little more. Before they knew it, she had drunk the whole glass down to the last drop.

"Mother," the nuns asked with earnest, "please give us some wisdom before you die."
She raised herself up in bed with a pious look on her face and said, "Don't sell that cow."

A priest and a nun are on their way back from the cemetery when their car breaks down.
The garage doesn't open until morning so they have to spend the night in a B&B. It only has one room available.
The priest says: "Sister, I don't think the Lord would object if we spend the night sharing this one room. I'll sleep on the sofa and you have the bed."
"I think that would be fine," agrees the nun.
They prepare for bed, say some prayers and settle down to sleep.
Ten minutes pass, and the nun says: "Father, I'm very cold."
"OK," says the priest, "I'll get a blanket from the cupboard."
Another ten minutes pass and the nun says again: "Father, I'm still terribly cold."
The priest says: "Don't worry, I'll get up and fetch you another blanket."
Another ten minutes pass, then the nun murmurs softly: "Father I'm still very cold. I don't think the Lord would mind if we acted as man and wife just for a night."

"You're right," says the priest. "Get your own blankets."

It was the end of the Gulf war. The Arabs stared over at the Oil Fields and watched them burning. Day and Night the Flames roared into the sky. The Arabs pondered on how they were going to put out the fires when one Arab suggested that they ring 'Red O Dare'. Red O Dare was contacted but informed the Arabs that he was busy for the next six months. Red O Dare told the Arabs that they should ring his cousin Paddy O Dare from Co Mayo in Ireland.

The Arab got on the phone and contacted Paddy. The Arab explained the problem with the Oil Fields to Paddy and asked if he could help. Paddy Replied: "No Problem." The Arab asked him how quick he could get there and how much would it cost?.

Paddy Replied: "I can be there in 10 Hours and it'll cost ya' $10,000. "Great"; said the Arab and hung up the phone.

The Arabs waited in the Desert, still watching the flames shooting into the sky, when all of a sudden an open top truck with four Irishmen inside comes roaring over the Sand Dunes and heads straight into the oil field.

The Arabs shouted to no avail, and the truck drove straight into one of the burning rigs. They jumped out, took off their Denim Jackets and proceeded to beat the fire out with them. The Arabs watched with amazement and two days later the Oil Rig Fire was Out. The four Paddy's walked to the Arabs and one said...."Jazus..that was rough!".

The Arab, while writing the check for $10,000, said to Paddy; "And what are you going to buy with all this money?. "Paddy Replied: "Well, the first thing I'm going to do is buy a set of brakes for that truck!!"

A man stumbles up to the only other patron in a bar and asks if he could buy him a drink.

"Why of course," comes the reply.

The first man then asks: "Where are you from?"

"I'm from Ireland," replies the second man.

The first man responds: "You don't say, I'm from Ireland too! Let's have another round to Ireland."

"Of Course," replies the second man.

Curious, the first man then asks: "Where in Ireland are you from?"

"Dublin," comes the reply.

"I can't believe it," says the first man. "I'm from Dublin too! Let's have another drink to Dublin."

"Of course," replies the second man.

Curiosity again strikes and the first man asks: "What school did you go to?"

"Saint Mary's," replies the second man. "I graduated in '62."

"This is unbelievable!" the first man says. "I went to Saint Mary's and I graduated in '62, too!"

About that time in comes one of the regulars and sits down at the bar. "What's been going on?" he asks the bartender.

"Nothing much," replies the bartender. "The O'Malley twins are drunk again."

McQuillan walked into a bar and ordered martini after martini, each time removing the olives and placing them in a jar. When the jar was filled with olives and all the drinks consumed, he started to leave.

"S'cuse me," said a customer, who was puzzled over what McQuillan had done. "What was that all about?"

"Nothing," he replied, "my wife just sent me out for a jar of olives."

Paddy the Drunk

The priest met him one day, and gave him a strong lecture about drink, hoping to scare the bejeezus out of him. He said, "If you continue drinking as you do, you'll gradually get smaller and smaller, and eventually you'll turn into a mouse." This frightened the life out of Paddy. He went home that night, and said to his wife, "Bridget.... if you should notice me getting smaller and smaller, will ye kill that blasted cat?"

Three Irish nuns were talking one sunny day in June.

The first nun said, "I was cleaning in Father's Murphy's room the other day and do you know what I found? A bottle of whiskey and a bunch of pornographic magazines!"

"What did you do?" the other nuns asked.

"Well, of course I threw the whiskey and the whore magazines in the trash," she replied.

The second nun said, "Well, I can top that. I was in Father's Murphy's room putting away the laundry and I found a box of condoms!"

"Oh my!" gasped the other nuns. "What did you do?" they asked.

"I poked holes in all of them!" she replied.

The Third nun fainted.

An attractive blonde from Cork, Ireland arrived at the casino. She seemed a little intoxicated and bet twenty-thousand Euros on a single roll of the dice. She said, 'I hope you don't mind, but I feel much luckier when I'm completely nude'. With that, she stripped from the neck down, rolled the dice and with an Irish brogue yelled, 'Come on, baby, Mama needs new clothes!' As the dice came to a stop, she jumped up and down and squealed...'YES! YES! I WON, I WON!' She hugged each of the dealers and then picked up her winnings and her clothes and quickly departed.

The dealers stared at each other dumbfounded.

Finally, one of them asked, 'What did she roll?'

The other answered, 'I don't know - I thought you were watching.'

MORAL OF THE STORY -

Not all Irish are drunks, not all blondes are dumb, but all men...are men.

A woman and a man driver are involved in a horrific collision, but amazingly both escape completely unhurt - though their cars are written off.

As they crawl out of the wreckage, the man sees the woman is blonde and strikingly beautiful. Then the woman turns to the man and gushes breathily:

'That's incredible - both our cars are demolished but we're fine. It must be a sign from God that we are meant to be together!'

Sensing a promise, the man stammers back, 'Oh yes, I agree with you completely!'

The woman goes on, 'And look, though my car was destroyed, this bottle of wine survived intact, too! It must be another sign. Let's drink to our love!'

'Well, OK!' says the man, going with the moment. She offers him the bottle, so he downs half of it and hands it back.

'Your turn,' says the man.

'No, thanks,' says the woman, 'I think I'll just wait for the police.'

Actual Personal ad from the Dublin News
"Heavy drinker,35, Cork area. Seeks gorgeous woman interested in a
man who loves his pints, cigarettes, Glasgow Celtic Football Club and
starting fights on Patrick Street at three o'clock in the morning"

Pat and Mick landed themselves a job at a sawmill in Ireland. Just before morning tea Pat yelled:
"Mick! I lost me finger!"
"How did you do it?" Mick asked
"I just touched this big spinning thing here like this... Damn! There goes another one!"

Two Irishmen, Patrick Murphy and Shawn O'Brian grew up together and were lifelong friends. But alas, Patrick developed cancer, and was dying. While on his deathbed, Patrick called to his buddy, Shawn, "O'Brian, come 'ere. I 'ave a request for ye." Shawn walked to his friend's bedside and kneels.

"Shawny ole boy, we've been friends all our lives, and now I'm leaving 'ere. I 'ave one last request fir ye to do."

O'Brian burst into tears, "Anything Patrick, anything ye wish. It's done."

"Well, under me bed is a box containing a bottle of the finest whiskey in all of Ireland. Bottled the year I was born it was. After I die, and they plant me in the ground, I want you to pour that fine whiskey over me grave so it might soak into me bones and I'll be able to enjoy it for all eternity."

O'Brian was overcome by the beauty and in the true Irish spirit of his friend's request, he asked, "Aye, tis a fine thing you ask of me, and I will pour the whiskey. But, might I strain it through me kidneys first?"

There was once an Irishman named Murphy who walked into an American Bar. He sat down and asked the Bartender "Give me three shots o' your finest Irish Whiskey!" the Bartender complies.

After about a week the bartender asks, "Murphy, would it be better for yeh if I put all three shots of Irish Whiskey into one glass?"

Murphy replied, "well no. See I have two other brothers back at home, Patrick and Owen, and everytime I come into a Pub or Bar I order a shot for each o' them so I can remember the good times."

Well, after another week of this routine, Murphy comes into the bar and only asks for two shots of Irish Whiskey. The bartender immediately says "Murphy, is everything ok? Did somethin' happen to one of your brothers?" "Oh no", Murphy said, "I just decided to quit drinkin!"

Two nuns, Sister Marilyn and Sister Helen, are traveling through Europe in their car. They get to Transylvania and are stopped at a traffic light. Suddenly, out of nowhere, a diminutive Dracula jumps onto the hood of the car and hisses through the windshield.

"Turn the windshield wipers on. That will get rid of the abomination," says Sister Helen.

Sister Marilyn switches them on, knocking Dracula about, but he clings on and continues hissing at the nuns. "What shall I do now?" she shouts.

Sister Marilyn turned on the windshield washer. Dracula screams as the water burns his skin, but he clings on and continues hissing at the nuns. "Now what?" shouts Sister Marilyn.

"Show him your cross," says Sister Helen.

"Now you're talking," says Sister Marilyn as she opens the window and shouts, "Get the fuck off our car!"

A garda pulls over a speeding car. He says, "I clocked you at 80 miles per hour, sir." The driver says, "Are you sure? I had it on cruise control at 60, perhaps your radar gun needs calibrating." Not looking up from her knitting the wife says: "Now don't be silly dear, you know that this car doesn't have cruise control." As the garda writes out the ticket, the driver looks over at his wife and growls, "Can't you please keep your mouth shut for once?" The wife smiles demurely and says, "You should be thankful your radar detector went off when it did." As the garda makes out the second ticket for the illegal use of a radar detector unit*, the man glowers at his wife and says through clenched teeth, "Woman ,didn't I tell you to keep your mouth shut!" The garda frowns and says "And I notice that you're not wearing your seat belt, sir. That's an on the spot 60 euro fine. "The driver says, "Well, you see sir, I had it on, but took it off when you pulled me over so that I could get my license out of my back pocket." The wife says, "Now, dear, you know very well that you didn't have your seat belt on. You never wear your seat belt when you're driving." And as the garda is writing out the third ticket the driver turns to his wife and barks, "WHY DON'T YOU PLEASE SHUT UP??" The garda looks over at the woman and asks, "Does your husband always talk to you this way, Ma'am?" Smiling sweetly, she replies. Only when he's been drinking, sir."

Miss O'Leary, the church organist, was in her eighties and had never been married. She was much admired for her sweetness and kindness to all. The parish priest came to call on her one afternoon early in the spring, and she welcomed him into her little cottage. She invited him to have a seat while she made the tea. As he sat facing her old pump organ, the priest noticed a cut glass bowl sitting on top of it, filled with water. In the water floated, of all things, an item the menfolk use to help prevent conception. Imagine his shock and surprise. Imagine his curiosity! Surely Miss O'Leary had lost her senses! When she returned with the tea and scones, they began to chat. The priest tried to stifle his curiosity about the bowl of water and its unusual contents, but soon it got the better of him; he could resist no longer. Miss O'Leary," he said, "I wonder if you would tell me about this?" (pointing to the bowl). "Oh, yes, Father," she replied, "Isn't it wonderful? I was walking in the village last October and I found this little package on the ground. The directions said to put it on the organ, keep it wet, and it would prevent disease. And you know... I haven't had a cold all winter.

Miss O'Leary, the church organist, was in her eighties and had never been married. She was much admired for her sweetness and kindness to all. The parish priest came to call on her one afternoon early in the spring, and she welcomed him into her little cottage. She invited him to have a seat while she made the tea. As he sat facing her old pump organ, the priest noticed a cut glass bowl sitting on top of it, filled with water. In the water floated, of all things, an item the menfolk use to help prevent conception. Imagine his shock and surprise. Imagine his curiosity! Surely Miss O'Leary had lost her senses! When she returned with the tea and scones, they began to chat. The priest tried to stifle his curiosity about the bowl of water and its unusual contents, but soon it got the better of him; he could resist no longer. Miss O'Leary," he said, "I wonder if you would tell me about this?" (pointing to the bowl). "Oh, yes, Father," she replied, "Isn't it wonderful? I was walking in the village last October and I found this little package on the ground. The directions said to put it on the organ, keep it wet, and it would prevent disease. And you know... I haven't had a cold all winter.

A woman awakes during the night to find that her husband was not in their bed. She puts on her robe and goes downstairs to look for him. She finds him sitting at the kitchen table with a cup of coffee in front of him. He appears deep in thought, just staring at the wall. She watches as he wipes a tear from his eye and takes a sip of coffee. "What's the matter, dear?" she whispers as she steps into the room, "Why are you down here at this time of night?" Do you remember when I met you and you were only 16?" he asks solemnly. The wife is touched to tears thinking that her husband is so caring and sensitive. "Yes, I do" she replies. The husband pauses. The words are not coming easily. "Do you remember when your father caught us in the back seat of my car, making love?" "Yes, I remember" says the wife, lowering herself into a chair beside him. The husband continues... "Do you remember when he shoved a shotgun in my face and said, "Either you marry my daughter, or I will send you to jail for 20 years?'" "I remember that too" she replies softly. He wipes another tear from his cheek and says..."I would have gotten out today."

The rich American couldn't understand why the Irish angler was lying lazily beside his boat on the beach, smoking a pipe. "Why aren't you out fishing?" asked the American. "Because I have caught enough fish for the day," said the fisherman. "Why don't you catch some more?" "What would I do with them?" "You could sell them and make more money," was the American's reply. "With that you could have a motor fixed to your boat and go into deeper waters and catch more fish. Then you would make enough to buy nets. These would bring you more fish and more money. Soon you would have enough money to own two boats . . . maybe even a fleet of boats. Then you would be a rich man like me." "What would I do then?" asked the fisherman. "Then you could really enjoy life." said the American. "And what do you suppose I might be doing right now?" said the Irishman, smiling and puffing away on his pipe.

Sean was a mild-mannered man who was tired of being hen-pecked by his wife; so he went to a psychiatrist. The psychiatrist said he needed to build his self-esteem and gave him a book on assertiveness. Sean read the book on the bus home. By the time he reached his house, he had finished it. He stormed into the house and walked up to his wife. Pointing a finger in her face, he said, "Bridie, from now on, I want you to know that I am the man of the house, and my word is law! I want you to make my favourite boiled beef and cabbage for the meal tonight and when I'm finished with that, I expect my favourite whiskey cake for afters. Then, you're going to draw me my bath so I can relax. And when I'm finished with that, do you know who's going to dress me and comb my hair?" "The undertaker." says she.

After just a few years of marriage filled with constant bickering, the Kerry couple decided the only way to save their marriage was to try counseling. When they arrived at the counselor's office, the counselor jumped right in and opened the floor for discussion. "What seems to be the problem?" Immediately, the husband held his long face down without anything to say. In contrast, the wife began talking 90 miles an hour, describing all the wrongs within their marriage. After 15 minutes of listening to the wife, the counselor went over to her, picked her up by her shoulders, kissed her passionately and sat her back down. Afterwards, the wife sat speechless. The marriage counselor looked over at the husband, who stared in disbelief. The counselor said to the husband, "Your wife NEEDS that at least twice a week!" The husband scratched his head and replied, "I can have her here on Tuesdays and Thursdays."

Sean calls home to his wife and says, "Aiofe, I have been asked to go fishing on Lough Ree with my boss and several of his friends. We'll be gone for a week. This is a good opportunity for me to get that promotion I've been wanting so would you please pack me enough clothes for a week and set out my rod and tackle box. We're leaving from the office and I'll stop by the house to pick them up. Oh, and, please pack my new blue silk pajamas."

A woman goes to the post office to stock up on stamps. She says to the clerk, "May I have 50 stamps please? The clerk says, "What denomination?" The woman says, "God bless us, has it come to that? I'll have 18 Protestants, and 32 Catholics."

An elderly Kerry couple is sitting together watching television. During one of 'those' commercials, the husband asked his wife, "Whatever happened to our sexual relations?" After a long thoughtful silence (and during the next commercial), the wife replied, "You know, I don't know. I don't even think we got a Christmas card from them this year.

Maureen's husband, Patrick, was a typical Irish male chauvinist. Even though they both worked full-time, he never helped around the house. Housework was woman's work! But one evening, Maureen arrived home to find the children bathed, one load of clothes in the washer and another in the dryer, dinner on the stove, and the table set. She was astonished; something's up, she thought.

It turns out that Patrick had read an article that said wives who worked full-time and also had to do all the housework were too tired to make love.

The night went well and the next day she told her office friends all about it. "We had a great dinner. Patrick even cleaned up. He helped the kids do their homework, folded all the laundry and put everything away. I really enjoyed the evening." "But what about afterward?" asked her friends. "Oh, that was perfect, too. Patrick was too tired!"

A gorgeous young redhead goes into the doctor's office and says that her body hurts wherever she touches it. "Impossible!" says the doctor. "Show me." The redhead takes her finger, pushes on her left breast and screams, then she pushes her elbow and screams in even more agony. She pushes her knee and screams; likewise she pushes her ankle and screams. Everywhere she touches makes her scream. The doctor says, "You're not really a redhead, are you? "Well, no" she says, "I'm actually a blonde." "I thought so," the doctor says. "Your finger is broken."

Mrs. O'Leary went to the doctor's office where she was seen by one of the new physicians. After about 4 minutes in the examination room, she burst out the door and ran screaming down the hall. An older doctor stopped her and asked what the problem was, and she told him her story. After listening, he had her sit down and relax in another room. The older doctor marched down the hallway to the back where the first doctor was and demanded, "What's the matter with you? Mrs. O'Leary is 72 years old, she has seven grown children and ten grandchildren, and you told her she was pregnant?" The new doctor continued to write on his clipboard and without looking up said, "Does she still have the hiccups?"

Costigan from Cork was marooned on a desert island where he was looked after by a beautiful native girl. On the first night she gave him exotic drinks. On the second night she gave him the most delicious food. On the third night she said to him coyly "Would you like to play a little game with me?" "Don't tell me," he says, "you have hurling here as well?"

One morning at the bargaining table, the company's chief negotiator held aloft the morning edition of the Cork Examiner. "This man," he announced, "Called in sick yesterday!" There on the sports page was a photo of the supposedly ill employee, who had just won a local golf tournament with an excellent score. The silence in the room was broken by a union negotiator. "Jaysus," he said. "Think of the score he could have had if he hadn't been sick!"

A Kerry man went for a job at the local stables and the farmer said "Can you shoe horses?" The Kerry man thinks for a minute and then says "No,but I once told a donkey to get lost."

A teacher was testing the children in her Sunday school class to see if they understood the concept of getting into heaven. She asked them, "If I sold my house and my car, had a big rummage sale and gave all my money to the church, would that get me into Heaven?" "NO!" the children answered. "If I cleaned the church every day, cut the grass, and kept everything tidy, would that get me into Heaven?" Again, the answer was, "NO!" By now the teacher was starting to smile - this was fun! "Well, then, if I was kind to animals and gave sweets to all the children, and loved my husband, would that get me into Heaven?" Again, they all answered, "NO!" Bursting with pride for them, the teacher continued: "So, how can I get into Heaven?" Five-year-old Sean shouted out, "YOU HAVE TO BE DEAD."

John Smith was the only Protestant to move into a large Catholic neighborhood. On the first Friday of Lent, John was outside grilling a big juicy steak on his grill. Meanwhile, all of his neighbors were fixing fish. This went on each Friday of Lent. On the last Friday of Lent, the neighborhood men got together and decided that something had to be done about John - he was tempting them to eat meat each Friday of Lent, and they couldn't take it anymore. They decided to try and convert John to be a Catholic. They went over and talked to him and were so happy that he decided to join all of his neighbors and become a Catholic. They took him to Church, and the Priest sprinkled some water over him, and said, "You were born a Baptist, you were raised a Baptist, and now you are a Catholic." The men were so relieved, now their biggest Lenten temptation was resolved. The next year's Lenten season rolled around. The first Friday of Lent came, and just at supper time, when the neighborhood was sitting down to their fish dinner, came the wafting smell of steak cooking on a grill. The neighborhood men could not believe their noses! WHAT WAS GOING ON? They called each other up and decided to meet over at John's place to see if he had forgotten it was the first Friday of Lent. The group arrived just in time to see John standing over his grill with a small pitcher of water. He was sprinkling some water over his steak on the grill, saying, "You were born a cow, you were raised a cow, and now you are a fish."

A Kerryman was playing Trivial Pursuit. It was his turn. He rolled the dice and landed on "Science & Nature." His question was, "If you are in a vacuum and someone calls your name, can you hear it?" He thought for a time and then asked, "Is it on or off?"

It was the end of the Gulf war. The Arabs stared over at the Oil Fields and watched them burning. Day and Night the Flames roared into the sky. The Arabs pondered on how they were going to put out the fires when one Arab suggested that they ring 'Red O Dare'. Red O Dare was contacted but informed the Arabs that he was busy for the next six months. Red O Dare told the Arabs that they should ring his cousin Paddy O Dare from Co Mayo in Ireland. The Arab got on the phone and contacted Paddy. The Arab explained the problem with the Oil Fields to Paddy and asked if he could help. Paddy Replied: "No Problem." The Arab asked him how quick he could get there and how much would it cost?. Paddy Replied: "I can be there in 10 Hours and it'll cost ya' $10,000. "Great"; said the Arab and hung up the phone. The Arabs waited in the Desert, still watching the flames shooting into the sky, when all of a sudden an open top truck with four Irishmen inside comes roaring over the Sand Dunes and heads straight into the oil field. The Arabs shouted to no avail, and the truck drove straight into one of the burning rigs. They jumped out, took off their Denim Jackets and proceeded to beat the fire out with them. The Arabs watched with amazement and two days later the Oil Rig Fire was Out. The four Paddy's walked to the Arabs and one said...."Jazus..that was rough!". The Arab, while writing the check for $10,000, said to Paddy; "And what are you going to buy with all this money?. "Paddy Replied: "Well, the first thing I'm going to do is buy a set of brakes for that truck!!"

A man stumbles up to the only other patron in a bar and asks if he could buy him a drink.

"Why of course," comes the reply.

The first man then asks: "Where are you from?"

"I'm from Ireland," replies the second man.

The first man responds: "You don't say, I'm from Ireland too! Let's have another round to Ireland."

"Of Course," replies the second man.

Curious, the first man then asks: "Where in Ireland are you from?"

"Dublin," comes the reply.

"I can't believe it," says the first man. "I'm from Dublin too! Let's have another drink to Dublin."

"Of course," replies the second man.

Curiosity again strikes and the first man asks: "What school did you go to?"

"Saint Mary's," replies the second man. "I graduated in '62."

"This is unbelievable!" the first man says. "I went to Saint Mary's and I graduated in '62, too!"

About that time in comes one of the regulars and sits down at the bar. "What's been going on?" he asks the bartender.

"Nothing much," replies the bartender. "The O'Malley twins are drunk again."

McQuillan walked into a bar and ordered martini after martini, each time removing the olives and placing them in a jar. When the jar was filled with olives and all the drinks consumed, he started to leave.

"S'cuse me," said a customer, who was puzzled over what McQuillan had done. "What was that all about?"

"Nothing," he replied, "my wife just sent me out for a jar of olives."

The priest met him one day, and gave him a strong lecture about drink, hoping to scare the bejeezus out of him. He said, "If you continue drinking as you do, you'll gradually get smaller and smaller, and eventually you'll turn into a mouse." This frightened the life out of Paddy. He went home that night, and said to his wife, "Bridget.... if you should notice me getting smaller and smaller, will ye kill that blasted cat?"

Three Irish nuns were talking one sunny day in June.

The first nun said, "I was cleaning in Father's Murphy's room the other day and do you know what I found? A bottle of whiskey and a bunch of pornographic magazines!"

"What did you do?" the other nuns asked.

"Well, of course I threw the whiskey and the whore magazines in the trash," she replied.

The second nun said, "Well, I can top that. I was in Father's Murphy's room putting away the laundry and I found a box of condoms!"

"Oh my!" gasped the other nuns. "What did you do?" they asked.

"I poked holes in all of them!" she replied.

The Third nun fainted.

An attractive blonde from Cork, Ireland arrived at the casino. She seemed a little intoxicated and bet twenty-thousand Euros on a single roll of the dice. She said, 'I hope you don't mind, but I feel much luckier when I'm completely nude'. With that, she stripped from the neck down, rolled the dice and with an Irish brogue yelled, 'Come on, baby, Mama needs new clothes!' As the dice came to a stop, she jumped up and down and squealed...'YES! YES! I WON, I WON!' She hugged each of the dealers and then picked up her winnings and her clothes and quickly departed.

The dealers stared at each other dumbfounded. Finally, one of them asked, 'What did she roll?' The other answered, 'I don't know - I thought you were watching.'

MORAL OF THE STORY -

Not all Irish are drunks, not all blondes are dumb, but all men...are men.

A woman and a man driver are involved in a horrific collision, but amazingly both escape completely unhurt - though their cars are written off.

As they crawl out of the wreckage, the man sees the woman is blonde and strikingly beautiful. Then the woman turns to the man and gushes breathily: 'That's incredible - both our cars are demolished but we're fine. It must be a sign from God that we are meant to be together!'

Sensing a promise, the man stammers back, 'Oh yes, I agree with you completely!'

The woman goes on, 'And look, though my car was destroyed, this bottle of wine survived intact, too! It must be another sign. Let's drink to our love!'

'Well, OK!' says the man, going with the moment. She offers him the bottle, so he downs half of it and hands it back.

'Your turn,' says the man.

'No, thanks,' says the woman, 'I think I'll just wait for the police.'

How can you possibly not love the Irish?

Actual Personal ad from the Dublin News

"Heavy drinker,35, Cork area. Seeks gorgeous woman interested in a

man who loves his pints, cigarettes, Glasgow Celtic Football Club and

starting fights on Patrick Street at three o'clock in the morning"

Pat and Mick landed themselves a job at a sawmill in Ireland. Just before morning tea Pat yelled:

"Mick! I lost me finger!"

"How did you do it?" Mick asked

"I just touched this big spinning thing here like this... Damn! There goes another one!"

Two Irishmen, Patrick Murphy and Shawn O'Brian grew up together and were lifelong friends. But alas, Patrick developed cancer, and was dying. While on his deathbed, Patrick called to his buddy, Shawn, "O'Brian, come 'ere. I 'ave a request for ye." Shawn walked to his friend's bedside and kneels. "Shawny ole boy, we've been friends all our lives, and now I'm leaving 'ere. I 'ave one last request fir ye to do."

O'Brian burst into tears, "Anything Patrick, anything ye wish. It's done."

"Well, under me bed is a box containing a bottle of the finest whiskey in all of Ireland. Bottled the year I was born it was. After I die, and they plant me in the ground, I want you to pour that fine whiskey over me grave so it might soak into me bones and I'll be able to enjoy it for all eternity."

O'Brian was overcome by the beauty and in the true Irish spirit of his friend's request, he asked, "Aye, tis a fine thing you ask of me, and I will pour the whiskey. But, might I strain it through me kidneys first?"

There was once an Irishman named Murphy who walked into an American Bar. He sat down and asked the Bartender "Give me three shots o' your

finest Irish Whiskey!" the Bartender complies.
After about a week the bartender asks, "Murphy,
would it be better for yeh if I put all three shots of
Irish Whiskey into one glass?"
Murphy replied, "well no. See I have two other
brothers back at home, Patrick and Owen, and
everytime I come into a Pub or Bar I order a shot
for each o' them so I can remember the good
times."

Well, after another week of this routine, Murphy
comes into the bar and only asks for two shots of
Irish Whiskey. The bartender immediately says
"Murphy, is everything ok? Did somethin' happen
to one of your brothers?" "Oh no", Murphy said, "I
just decided to quit drinkin!"

Two nuns, Sister Marilyn and Sister Helen, are
traveling through Europe in their car. They get to
Transylvania and are stopped at a traffic light.
Suddenly, out of nowhere, a diminutive Dracula
jumps onto the hood of the car and hisses through
the windshield.

"Turn the windshield wipers on. That will get rid of
the abomination," says Sister Helen.
Sister Marilyn switches them on, knocking Dracula
about, but he clings on and continues hissing at the
nuns. "What shall I do now?" she shouts.
Sister Marilyn turned on the windshield washer.
Dracula screams as the water burns his skin, but he
clings on and continues hissing at the nuns. "Now
what?" shouts Sister Marilyn.
"Show him your cross," says Sister Helen.

"Now you're talking," says Sister Marilyn as she opens the window and shouts, "Get the fuck off our car!"

Miss O'Leary, the church organist, was in her eighties and had never been married. She was much admired for her sweetness and kindness to all. The parish priest came to call on her one afternoon early in the spring, and she welcomed him into her little cottage. She invited him to have a seat while she made the tea. As he sat facing her old pump organ, the priest noticed a cut glass bowl sitting on top of it, filled with water. In the water floated, of all things, an item the menfolk use to help prevent conception. Imagine his shock and surprise. Imagine his curiosity! Surely Miss O'Leary had lost her senses! When she returned with the tea and scones, they began to chat. The priest tried to stifle his curiosity about the bowl of water and its unusual contents, but soon it got the better of him; he could resist no longer. Miss O'Leary," he said, "I wonder if you would tell me about this?" (pointing to the bowl). "Oh, yes, Father," she replied, "Isn't it wonderful? I was walking in the village last October and I found this little package on the ground. The directions said to put it on the organ, keep it wet, and it would prevent disease. And you know... I haven't had a cold all winter.

An unfortunate slip recently occurred at a wedding breakfast in Killarney, Co. Kerry. The happy pair had been toasted in the usual way. Then a general conversation took place, which related to the nuisance of children being present at social gatherings - especially weddings. A happy idea struck the bridegroom. "Why not have it mentioned on the invitation cards?" said he. "For instance, we could have had on ours No Children Expected." A long silence followed, until somebody remarked that the weather was remarkable for this time of year.

A woman awakes during the night to find that her husband was not in their bed. She puts on her robe and goes downstairs to look for him. She finds him sitting at the kitchen table with a cup of coffee in front of him. He appears deep in thought, just staring at the wall. She watches as he wipes a tear from his eye and takes a sip of coffee. "What's the matter, dear?" she whispers as she steps into the room, "Why are you down here at this time of night?" Do you remember when I met you and you were only 16?" he asks solemnly. The wife is touched to tears thinking that her husband is so caring and sensitive. "Yes, I do" she replies. The husband pauses. The words are not coming easily.

"Do you remember when your father caught us in the back seat of my car, making love?" "Yes, I remember" says the wife, lowering herself into a chair beside him. The husband continues... "Do you remember when he shoved a shotgun in my face and said, "Either you marry my daughter, or I will send you to jail for 20 years?"" "I remember that too" she replies softly. He wipes another tear from his cheek and says..."I would have gotten out today."

Sean was a mild-mannered man who was tired of being hen-pecked by his wife; so he went to a psychiatrist. The psychiatrist said he needed to build his self-esteem and gave him a book on assertiveness. Sean read the book on the bus home. By the time he reached his house, he had finished it. He stormed into the house and walked up to his wife. Pointing a finger in her face, he said, "Bridie, from now on, I want you to know that I am the man of the house, and my word is law! I want you to make my favourite boiled beef and cabbage for the meal tonight and when I'm finished with that, I expect my favourite whiskey cake for afters. Then, you're going to draw me my bath so I can relax. And when I'm finished with that, do you know who's going to dress me and comb my hair?"
"The undertaker." says she.

After just a few years of marriage filled with constant bickering, the Kerry couple decided the only way to save their marriage was to try counseling. When they arrived at the counselor's office, the counselor jumped right in and opened the floor for discussion. "What seems to be the problem?" Immediately, the husband held his long face down without anything to say. In contrast, the wife began talking 90 miles an hour, describing all the wrongs within their marriage. After 15 minutes of listening to the wife, the counselor went over to her, picked her up by her shoulders, kissed her passionately and sat her back down. Afterwards, the wife sat speechless. The marriage counselor looked over at the husband, who stared in disbelief. The counselor said to the husband,"Your wife NEEDS that at least twice a week!" The husband scratched his head and replied, "I can have her here on Tuesdays and Thursdays."

Sean calls home to his wife and says, "Aiofe, I have been asked to go fishing on Lough Ree with my boss and several of his friends. We'll be gone for a week. This is a good opportunity for me to get that promotion I've been wanting so would you please pack me enough clothes for a week and set out my rod and tackle box. We're leaving from the office and I'll stop by the house to pick them up. Oh, and, please pack my new blue silk pajamas."

A woman goes to the post office to stock up on stamps. She says to the clerk, "May I have 50 stamps please? The clerk says, "What denomination?" The woman says, "God bless us, has it come to that? I'll have 18 Protestants, and 32 Catholics."

An elderly Kerry couple is sitting together watching television. During one of 'those' commercials, the husband asked his wife, "Whatever happened to our sexual relations?" After a long thoughtful silence (and during the next commercial), the wife replied, "You know, I don't know. I don't even think we got a Christmas card from them this year.

Maureen's husband, Patrick, was a typical Irish male chauvinist. Even though they both worked full-time, he never helped around the house. Housework was woman's work! But one evening, Maureen arrived home to find the children bathed, one load of clothes in the washer and another in the dryer, dinner on the stove, and the table set. She was astonished; something's up, she thought.

It turns out that Patrick had read an article that said wives who worked full-time and also had to do all the housework were too tired to make love. The night went well and the next day she told her office friends all about it. "We had a great dinner. Patrick even cleaned up. He helped the kids do their homework, folded all the laundry and put everything away. I really enjoyed the evening." "But what about afterward?" asked her friends. "Oh, that was perfect, too. Patrick was too tired!"

A gorgeous young redhead goes into the doctor's office and says that her body hurts wherever she touches it. "Impossible!" says the doctor. "Show me." The redhead takes her finger, pushes on her left breast and screams, then she pushes her elbow and screams in even more agony. She pushes her knee and screams; likewise she pushes her ankle and screams. Everywhere she touches makes her scream. The doctor says, "You're not really a redhead, are you? "Well, no" she says, "I'm actually a blonde." "I thought so," the doctor says. "Your finger is broken."

Mrs. O'Leary went to the doctor's office where she was seen by one of the new physicians. After about 4 minutes in the examination room, she burst out the door and ran screaming down the hall. An older doctor stopped her and asked what the problem was, and she told him her story. After listening, he had her sit down and relax in another room. The older doctor marched down the hallway to the back where the first doctor was and demanded, "What's the matter with you? Mrs. O'Leary is 72 years old, she has seven grown children and ten grandchildren, and you told her she was pregnant?" The new doctor continued to write on his clipboard and without looking up said, "Does she still have the hiccups?"

Costigan from Cork was marooned on a desert island where he was looked after by a beautiful native girl. On the first night she gave him exotic drinks. On the second night she gave him the most delicious food. On the third night she said to him coyly "Would you like to play a little game with me?" "Don't tell me," he says, "you have hurling here as well?"

One morning at the bargaining table, the company's chief negotiator held aloft the morning edition of the Cork Examiner. "This man," he announced, "Called in sick yesterday!" There on the sports page was a photo of the supposedly ill employee, who had just won a local golf tournament with an excellent score. The silence in the room was broken by a union negotiator."Jaysus," he said. "Think of the score he could have had if he hadn't been sick!"

A Kerry man went for a job at the local stables and the farmer said "Can you shoe horses?" The Kerry man thinks for a minute and then says "No,but I once told a donkey to get lost."

A teacher was testing the children in her Sunday school class to see if they understood the concept of getting into heaven. She asked them, "If I sold my house and my car, had a big rummage sale and gave all my money to the church, would that get me into Heaven?" "NO!" the children answered. "If I cleaned the church every day, cut the grass, and kept everything tidy, would that get me into Heaven?" Again, the answer was, "NO!" By now the teacher was starting to smile - this was fun! "Well, then, if I was kind to animals and gave sweets to all the children, and loved my husband, would that get me into Heaven?" Again, they all answered, "NO!" Bursting with pride for them, the teacher continued: "So, how can I get into Heaven?" Five-year-old Sean shouted out, "YOU HAVE TO BE DEAD."

John Smith was the only Protestant to move into a large Catholic neighborhood. On the first Friday of Lent, John was outside grilling a big juicy steak on his grill. Meanwhile, all of his neighbors were fixing fish. This went on each Friday of Lent. On the last Friday of Lent, the neighborhood men got together and decided that something had to be done about John - he was tempting them to eat meat each Friday of Lent, and they couldn't take it anymore. They decided to try and convert John to be a Catholic. They went over and talked to him and were so happy that he decided to join all of his neighbors and become a Catholic. They took him to Church, and the Priest sprinkled some water over him, and said, "You were born a Baptist, you were raised a Baptist, and now you are a Catholic." The men were so relieved, now their biggest Lenten temptation was resolved. The next year's Lenten season rolled around. The first Friday of Lent came, and just at supper time, when the neighborhood was sitting down to their fish dinner, came the wafting smell of steak cooking on a grill. The neighborhood men could not believe their noses! WHAT WAS GOING ON? They called each other up and decided to meet over at John's place to see if he had forgotten it was the first Friday of Lent. The group arrived just in time to see John standing over his grill with a small pitcher of water. He was sprinkling some water over his steak on the grill, saying, "You were born a cow, you were raised a cow, and now you are a fish."

A Kerryman was playing Trivial Pursuit. It was his turn. He rolled the dice and landed on "Science & Nature." His question was, "If you are in a vacuum and someone calls your name, can you hear it?" He thought for a time and then asked, "Is it on or off?"

Sean is walking through the park and notices an old lady sitting on a bench sobbing her eyes out. He stops and asks her what is wrong. She says, "I have a 22-year old husband at home. He kisses and cuddles me every morning and then gets up and makes me eggs, bacon, black pudding, toast and tea." Well then," Sean says, "Why are you crying?" She says, "He makes me homemade soup for lunch and then kisses and cuddles me for half the afternoon." Perplexed, Sean says, "So, why are you crying?" She says, "For supper, he always makes me my favourite meal and then kisses and cuddles me until 2:00 a.m. Astonished by now, Sean says, "Why in the world would you be crying, then?" Says she, "I can't remember where I live!"

Sean goes into the pub and asks for three Guinness. He sits there and sips from the first one, then the second, and the third. He does this until finally all three pints are finished. He pays the bill and leaves. A couple of nights later he comes back and repeats the ritual. This goes on for a while and finally the bartender's curiosity gets the better of him and he asks why the three Guinness and why drink them all together the way he does. "Well, " says Sean, "My brother Michael is in the USA and my other brother Liam is in Australia. We can't meet in the pub and share a Guinness, so we have an agreement that whenever we go have a drink, we order three pints and pretend we're together." The bartender thinks to himself, "What a wonderful idea." A few months go by and one night Sean comes in and he orders two Guinness. The bartender is afraid to ask, but Sean seems fine, so finally the bartender says, "I see you've only ordered two Guinness tonight. Did something happen to one of your brothers?"No, no," says Sean, "They're both fit as a fiddle and healthy as horses!" "So why only the two Guinness?" asks the bartender. "Ah, well now," says Sean, "I've given up Guinness for Lent."

A surgeon and an architect, both English, were joined by an Irish politician, and all fell to arguing as to whose profession was the oldest. Said the surgeon, "Eve was made from Adam's rib, and that surely was a surgical operation." "Maybe," said the architect, "but prior to that, order was created out of chaos, and that was an architectural job." "Sure now," interrupted the politician, "but wasn't somebody after creating the chaos first?"

A pompous priest was seated next to an Irishman on a flight home.
After the plane was airborne, drink orders were taken. The Irishman asked for an Irish whiskey. The attendant placed the drink on his tray and then asked the priest if he would like a drink. He replied in disgust," I'd rather be savagely ravaged by brazen hussies than let alcohol touch my lips."

The Irishman then handed his drink back to the attendant and said "Me
too. I didn't know we had a choice!"

Miss O'Leary, our lovely little old spinster from Leitrim makes a return visit this week. After Mass one Sunday, she went up to the priest and said, "I have to tell you Father, your sermons are a wonder to behold. Sure we didn't know what sin was till you came to the parish!"

The first priest says, "You know, since the warm weather started, I've been having trouble with mice in my church. I've tried everything - noise, cats, spray, nothing seems to scare them away." The second priest says, "My church, too. There are hundreds of them living in the cellar. I've set traps and even called in an expert exterminator. Nothing has worked so far." The third priest says, "I had the same problem. So I baptized them all and made them members of my parish. Haven't seen one of them since."

While impatiently waiting for a table in a restaurant, Miss O'Leary says to Mrs. Clancy, "If they weren't so crowded in here all the time, they'd do a lot more business."

A man walked into the lingerie department of Dunnes in Dublin and said to the woman behind the counter, "I'd like to buy a Baptist bra for my wife, size 36B." What type of bra? asked the clerk. "Baptist" said the man. She said get a Baptist bra, and that you'd know what she meant." "Ah yes, now I remember" said the saleslady. "We don't sell many of those. Mostly our customers want the Catholic type, the Salvation Army type. or the Presbyterian type."Confused the man asked, "What's the difference between them?" The lady responded, "It is all really quite simple; the Catholic type supports the masses, the Salvation Army type lifts up the fallen, and the Presbyterian type keeps them staunch and upright. Then there's the Baptist type." "What does that do?" asked the man. She replied, "It makes mountains out of molehills."

The spring bank holiday was over and the teacher asked the class how they had spent the time. Kevin eagerly put up his hand. "We visited our cousins in Carrigaline!" "Well, Kevin," says the teacher, "that sounds like a brilliant vocabulary word - can you tell the class how to spell Carrigaline?" Kevin furrowed his brow, chewed on his lip, and then said with a big grin, "Em, well now, come to think of it, we went to Cork!"

A man and a woman, who have never met before, find themselves assigned to the same sleeping room on a transcontinental train.Though initially embarrassed and uneasy over sharing a room, the two are tired and fall asleep quickly - he in the upper bunk and she in the lower. At 2:00AM, he leans over and gently wakes the woman, saying, "Ma'am, I'm sorry to bother you, but would you be willing to reach into the cupboard to get me a second blanket? I'm awfully cold." "I have a better idea," she replies. "Just for tonight, let's pretend that we're married." "That's a great idea!" he exclaims. "Good," she replies. "Get up and get your own blanket."

Two men walked into a pub late one afternoon and noticed that, among the few customers, was one individual sitting quietly at the end of the bar. The two ordered some beers. The bartender brought them and said, "that will be 50p please." They put it on the slate and a short time later ordered two more beers; again they were charged 25p each. The two could not believe the price and after having a third beer for the same amount, they decided to ask the bartender what the catch was. The bartender replied, "there is no catch, gentlemen. I have just started brewing this beer on the premises and I'm selling it below cost to introduce it to my customers. I'm happy to see you're enjoying it."

Indeed, they noticed that almost everyone was enjoying the beer and the remarkable price except for the one man at the end of the bar. He had not ordered anything since the two came in. Becoming very curious about this individual, the two asked the bartender, "Doesn't he ever order anything?" "Oh yes," said the bartender. "That's Patrick Curran, our local accountant. He's waiting for happy hour."

An Irishman died and went to heaven. As he stood in front of St. Peter at the Pearly Gates, he saw a huge wall of clocks behind him. He asked, "What are all those clocks?" St. Peter answered, "Those are Lie-Clocks. Everyone in the universe has a Lie-Clock. Every time you lie, the hands on your clock will move." "Oh," said the man, "whose clock is that?" "That's St. Patrick's. The hands have never moved, indicating that he never told a lie." "Incredible," said the man. "And whose clock is that one?" St. Peter responded, "That's Daniel O'Connell's clock. The hands have moved twice, telling us that he told only two lies in his entire life." "Where's Bertie Ahern's clock?" asked the man. "Bertie's clock is in God's office. He's using it as a ceiling fan."

Three men were sitting together bragging about how they had set their new wives straight on their domestic duties. The first man had married a woman from Italy and boasted that he had told his wife she was to do all the dishes and house cleaning that needed to be done. He said that it took a couple days but on the third day he came home to a clean house and the dishes were all washed and put away. The second man had married a woman from France. He bragged that he had given his wife orders that she was to do all the cleaning, all the dishes, and the cooking. He told them that the first day he didn't see any results, but the next day it was better. By the third day, his house was clean, the dishes were done, and he had a delicious dinner on the. table. The third man had married an Irish girl. He boasted that he told her his house was to be cleaned, the dishes washed, the cooking done and the laundry washed. And this was all entirely her responsibility. He said the first day he didn't see anything and the second day he didn't see anything, but by the third day some of the swelling had gone down so he could see a little out of his left eye!

A curious fellow died one day and found himself waiting in the long line of judgment. As he stood there he noticed that some souls were allowed to march right through the pearly gates into Heaven. Others though, were led over to Satan who threw them into the burning pit. But every so often, instead of hurling a poor soul into the fire, Satan would toss a soul off to one side into a small pile. After watching Satan do this several times, the fellow's curiosity got the best of him. So he strolled over and asked Satan what he was doing. "Excuse me, Prince of Darkness," he said. "I'm waiting in line for judgment, but I couldn't help wondering, why are you tossing those people aside instead of flinging them into the Fires of Hell with the others?" "Ah, those ...Satan said with a groan. "They're all from Ireland. They're still too cold and damp to burn."

The man from the window company called Miss O'Leary on the telephone. "Miss O'Leary, he says, you haven't made a single payment on your new windows. Is there something the matter?" Bristling with annoyance, Miss O'Leary replies. "I may be up in years, but I still have my wits about me. Wasn't your man after telling me those windows would pay for themselves in a year?"

Twins Jack and Sarah were always squabbling. Tired of listening to them yelling at each other and knowing full well neither one would admit they were in the wrong, their mother says, "I have an idea: Sarah, why don't you tell Jack you were wrong, and Jack, you tell Sarah she was right. So, Sarah says to Jack "I was wrong." Jack grins and says to Sarah: "You are right."

Two lovely old biddies had been friends for many decades. Over the years they had shared all kinds of activities and adventures. Lately, their activities had been limited to meeting a few times a week for a cup of tea and a natter. One day they were sipping their tea when one looked at the other and said, "Now don't go getting upset with me...I know we've been pals for a long time.....but I just can't think of your name! I've thought and thought, but I can't remember it. Please tell me what your name is. Her friend glared at her. For at least three minutes she just stared and glared. At last, she said, "How soon do you need to know?

A young lad had just gotten his provisional license. (learner's permit) He asked his father, who was a minister, if they could discuss his use of the car. His father said to him, "If you bring your marks up, study your bible, and get your hair cut, we'll talk about it." A month later the boy came back and again asked his father if they could now discuss his use of the car. His father said, "Well, son, I see that your marks have improved, you've studied your bible diligently, but you didn't get a hair cut!" The young man waited a moment and then replied, "You know dad, I've been thinking about that. Didn't Samson have long hair, Moses have long hair, Noah have long hair, and even Jesus himself have long hair?" His father replied, "They did so, and they walked everywhere they went!"

Morris walks out into the street and hails a taxi just going by. He gets into the taxi, and the cabbie says, "Perfect timing. You're just like Liam." "Who?" "Liam O'Connor. There's a lad who did everything right. Like my coming along when you needed a cab. It would have happened like that to Liam.""Every path has its puddle" says Morris." "It wasn't like that with Liam," says the cabbie."He was a brilliant athlete. He could have played football for Kerry. He could golf with the pros. He sang like Ronan Tynon and he danced like Michael Flatley. What's more, he had a memory like Methusalah. He could remember everyone's birthday. He knew all about wine, which fork to eat with. He could fix anything. Not like me. I change a fuse, and the whole town goes out.""No wonder you remember him." says Morris. "Well, I never actually met the man." "Then how do you know so much about him?" asks Morris. "I married his widow."

Mrs. Pete Monaghan came into the newsroom to pay for her husband's obituary. She was told by the kindly newsman that it was dollar a word and he remembered Pete and wasn't it too bad about him passing away. She thanked him for his kind words and bemoaned the fact that she only had two dollars. But she wrote out the obituary, "Pete died." The newsman said he thought old Pete deserved more and he'd give her three more words at no charge. Mrs. Pete Monaghan thanked him and rewrote the obituary: "Pete died. Boat for sale"

Pat and Mike are drinking in the done-up version of their local pub, The Continental Bistro and Bar in the Ballybegorrah Arms Hotel, Killarney. They take in the no-sawdust on the new Italian tile floor; the hi-back red leather bar stools; the bowls of free black olives, cashew nuts and tasty "tapas" on the shiny, black, two inch thick, granite counter. "Ye know", Pat," says Mike, "it's all brilliant, but I miss the auld spittoon." Pat takes his pipe from his mouth, sips his pint, then says,"You always did, me auld friend. You always did."

While working on a lesson in world religions, a kindergarten teacher asked her students to bring something related to their family's faith to class. At the appropriate time, she asked the students to come forward and share with the rest of the students. The first child said, "I am Muslim, and this is my prayer rug."

The second child said, "I am Jewish, and this is my Star of David."

The third child said, "I am Catholic, and this is my rosary."

The final child said, "I am Protestant, and this is my casserole dish.

An Irish lady goes to the bar on a cruise ship and orders a Jameson with two drops of water. As the bartender gives her the drink she says, "I'm on this cruise to celebrate my 80th birthday and it's today." The bartender says, "Well, since it's your birthday, I'll buy you a drink. In fact, this one is on me." "Well, thank you kindly, sir" says she. As the woman finishes her drink, the woman to her right says, "I would like to buy you a drink, too." The old woman says, "Thank you. Bartender, I'll have a Jameson with two drops of water." "Coming up," says the bartender. As she finishes that drink, the man to her left says, "I would like to buy you one, too." The old woman says, "Thank you. Bartender, I'll have another Jameson with two drops of water." "Coming right up," the bartender says. As he gives her the drink, he says, "Ma'am, I'm dying of curiosity. Why the Jameson with only two drops of water?" The old woman replies, "Ah, lad, when you're my age, you've learned how to hold the hard stuff. Holding your water, however, is another matter entirely."

Q: How many Irishmen does it take to change a light bulb?
A: Three. One to hold the bulb, one to screw it in, and one to say how grand the old one was.

Father Murphy went out one Saturday to visit his parishioners. At one house it was obvious that someone was home, but nobody came to the door even though the priest had knocked several times. Finally, he took out his card and wrote "Revelations 3:20" on the back of it, and stuck it in the door: "Behold, I stand at the door and knock. If anyone hears my voice and opens the door, I will come in to him and dine with him and him with me." The next day, the card turned up in the collection plate. Below Father Murphy's message was the notation "Genesis 3:10": "I heard your voice in the garden and I was afraid because I was naked; and I hid myself."

A man was brought to Mercy Hospital, and taken quickly in for coronary surgery. The operation went well and, as the groggy man regained consciousness, he was reassured by a Sister of Mercy, who was waiting by his bed. "Mr. O'Toole, you're going to be just fine," said the nun, gently patting his hand. "We do need to know, however, how you intend to pay for your stay here. Are you covered by insurance?" "No, sorry, I don't have any insurance," the man whispered hoarsely. "Can you pay in cash?" asked the nun. "I'm afraid I cannot, Sister." "Well, do you have any close relatives?" the nun persisted. "Just my sister in America" he volunteered. "But she's a humble spinster nun." "Oh, I must correct you, Mr. O'Toole. Nuns are not 'spinsters;' they are married to God." "Wonderful," said O'Toole. "In that case, please send the bill to my brother-in-law."

Attending a wedding for the first time, a little girl whispered to her mother, "Why is the lady all dressed in white?" "Because white is the color of happiness, and today is the happiest day of her life.

The child thought about this for a moment, then said, "So why is the man wearing black?"

An elderly woman died last month. Having never married, she requested no male pallbearers. In her handwritten instructions for her memorial service, she wrote, "They wouldn't take me out while I was alive, I don't want them to take me out when I'm dead."

"Which is the first and most important sacrament?" asked the Catechism teacher. "Marriage", avowed Moira. "No, baptism is the first and most important sacrament," corrected the teacher. "Not in our family," retorted Moira, in a haughty voice. "We're decent people!"

Charlie was a regular visitor at the Galway Races. One afternoon he noticed an unusual sight. Right before the first race, a Catholic priest visited one of the horses in the stable area and gave it a blessing. Charlie watched the race very carefully, and sure enough the blessed horse came in first! Charlie followed the priest before the next race, and again he went to the stables and performed a similar procedure. Thinking there might be something to it, Charlie put a couple of euros on the blessed horse. Sure enough it came in by two lengths and Charlie won close to fifty euros! The priest continued the same procedure through the next few races and Charlie won each time. He was now ahead a thousand, so between races Charlie left the track, went to the bank and withdrew his life's savings. The biggest race of the day was the last one. Charlie followed the priest and watched which horse he blessed. He then went to the betting window and put every euro he owned on that horse to win. The race began. Down the stretch they came, and as they crossed the finish line, Charlie's pick was last! Devastated, he found the priest and told him that he had been watching him bless the horses all day, and they all became winners except the last horse on which he had bet his life savings. Charlie then asked, "What happened to the last horse which you blessed? Why didn't it win like the others?" "Ye must be a Protestant," sighed the priest. "The trouble is you can't tell the difference between a blessing and the last rites."

A wealthy couple from Texas were touring Ireland and found themselves in a tiny rural village at lunchtime. The only place serving food was a somewhat rustic looking cafe which in their opinion, had seen better days. Having no other choice, they carefully stepped over the pooch snoozing on the threshold and went inside. As they sat down, the husband frowned as he brushed some crumbs from his chair and his wife did likewise as she wiped the table with her napkin.The waitress came over and asked if they would like to see a menu. "No thanks," said the husband. "I'll just have a cup of tea with cream and sugar."I'll have the same", his wife said. "And please make sure the cup is clean." Unphased by the rudeness of the remark, the waitress smiled and marched off into the kitchen. A few minutes later, she was back."Two cups of tea," she announced in her lovely lilting Irish brogue..."And which one of you was it who wanted the clean cup?"

At every tea-break, Sean, the hod-carrier was always boasting to his older work-mate, Mike the brick- layer, that he was the better worker because he was stronger, faster, and younger. Mike stoically put up with the bragging until one day, he couldn't take it any more. "Well, Sean", he said, I'll bet a week's wages I can haul something in a wheelbarrow over to that building that you won't be able to wheel back." Sean laughed derisively and agreed to the bet. With that, Mike grabbed the handles of the wheelbarrow and told Sean to get in.

A man and his wife, now in their 60's, were celebrating their 40th wedding anniversary. On their special day, a good fairy came to them and said that because they had been such a devoted couple she would grant each of them a very special wish. The wife wished for a trip around the world with her husband. Whoosh! Immediately she had airline & cruise tickets in her hands. The man wished for a female companion, 30 years younger..... Whoosh! Immediately he turned ninety!!!

Katie and Moira are old friends. They have both been married to their husbands for a long time. Katie is upset because she thinks her husband doesn't find her attractive anymore. "As I get older he doesn't bother to look at me!" she complains to Moira. "What a pity," says Moira. As I get older my husband says I get more beautiful every day. "All well and good, says Katie, but your husband's an antique dealer!"

The concierge at a posh resort was often asked about the ski facilities. One day a couple who had just checked in after a long flight came by and asked me where the lift was. "Go down the hill," he told them, "out the door, past the pool, 200 yards down the block, and you'll see it on your right." Their tired faces suddenly looked even more exhausted until the man behind them spoke up. "They're from Ireland," he said. "I think they're looking for the elevator."

In Killarney, an American tourist sees a sign in front of a farmhouse: "Talking Dog for Sale." He rings the bell and the farmer tells him the dog is around the back. The tourist goes behind the house and sees a black mutt just sitting there "You talk?" he asks. "Indeed." the dog replies. "So, what's your story?" The mutt looks up and says, "Well, I discovered my gift of talking when I was very young and I wanted to be of help to humanity, so I told Interpol about my gift; in no time they had me flying from country to country, sitting in rooms with world leaders, because no one would believe a dog would be listening. I was one of their most valuable spies for eight years running. The jetting around really tired me out, and I knew I wasn't getting any younger. So I signed up for a job at the airport to do some undercover security work, mostly wandering near suspicious characters and eavesdropping. I uncovered some very shady dealings there and was awarded a ton of medals. Then I settled down, had a wife, a dozen or so puppies, and now I'm just retired." The tourist is amazed. He goes back and asks the farmer what he wants for the dog. The farmer says, "Ten euros, sir." The tourist sputters, "But that dog is incredible. Why on earth are you selling him so cheap?" The farmer shrugs and says "Ah well, sir, you, see, isn't he just the biggest liar this side of Croagh Patrick? He's done none of what he told ye."

Father Doyle was a clever speaker and a firm advocate of abstinence, the closure of pubs on Sundays, and a standard of morality that would ensure a warm welcome in Heaven. One Sunday morning, among his listeners was a young country girl who was new to the parish. She was deeply impressed with the priest's eloquent preaching. Indeed, so impressed that she included a few lines about him in her next letter home:
"I never get tired of listening to Father Doyle. He is such a lovely speaker, you'd swear that every word he says is true."

A Catholic priest, a Protestant minister, and a Jewish rabbi were discussing when life begins. "Life begins," said the priest, "at the moment of fertilization. That is when God instills the spark of life into the fetus." "We believe," said the minister, "that life begins at birth, because that is when the baby becomes an individual and is capable of making its own decisions and must learn about sin." "You're both wrong," said the rabbi. "Life begins when the children have graduated and moved out of the house."

Two Irish men are in a plane. The roof comes off! Mick says to Paddy, "If this plane turns upside down will we fall out??""No way Mick" says Paddy, "we'll still be best friends."

Three priests went for a ramble in the country. It was unusually hot for Ireland in September and before too long, they were sweating profusely. They came upon a small lake and since it was fairly secluded, they took off all their clothes and jumped into the water. Feeling refreshed, the trio decided to pick a few blackberries while enjoying their "freedom". As they were crossing an open area, they saw a group of ladies from the village coming towards them. Unable to get to their clothes in time, two of the priests covered their privates, but the third one covered his face while they ran for cover. After the ladies had left and the men got their clothes back on, the first two priests asked the third why he covered his face rather than his privates. "I don't know about you two," he replied, "but in my parish, it's my face they would recognize."

An Irishman, a Mexican and a blond guy were doing construction work on the roof of a skyscraper. They were eating lunch and the Irishman said, "Corned beef and cabbage. If I get corned beef and cabbage one more time for lunch I'm going to jump off this building." The Mexican opened his lunch box and exclaimed, "Burritos again! If I get burritos one more time I'm going to jump off, too." The blond opened his lunch and said, "Bologna again. If I get a bologna sandwich one more time, I'm jumping as well." The next day the Irishman opened his lunch box, saw corned beef and cabbage and jumped. The Mexican opened his lunch, saw a burrito and jumped. The blond guy opened his lunch, saw the bologna and jumped. At the funeral, the Irishman's wife was weeping. She said, "If I'd known how tired he was of corned beef and cabbage, I never would have given it to him again!" The Mexican's wife also wept and said, "I could have given him tacos or enchiladas! I didn't realize he was so bored with burritos." Everyone turned and stared at the blonde guy's wife... wait for it.........

Hey, don't look at me," she said, "He makes his own lunch."

The store manager, O'Reilly, heard Maryann his assistant tell a customer, "No mam, we haven't had any for a while, and it doesn't look as if we'll be getting any soon." O'Reilly was horrified and ran over to the customer and said, "Of course we'll have some soon. We placed an order last week." Then he took the assistant aside and said, "Never, never, say we're out of anything - say we've got it on order and it's coming. Now what was it she wanted?"
"Rain," said the assistant.

A mother was preparing pancakes for her sons, Kevin, 5, and Ryan, 3. The boys began to squabble over who would get the first pancake. Their mother saw the opportunity for a moral lesson. "If Jesus were sitting here, He would say, 'Let my brother have the first pancake, I can wait.'" Kevin turned to his younger brother and said, "Ryan, you be Jesus!"

Idly, the American tourist watched the Cork man dig and turn over the soil. Eventually he called out: "Hey, buddy, what's that you're doing?"

"I'm digging potatoes, sir." "Potatoes? You call those puny things potatoes? Back home in Idaho we have potatoes ten times that size!" "Indeed sir, and that's as it needs be; a good potato should be of a size to fit the mouth."

A dietitian was addressing a large audience in Dublin. "The material we put into our stomachs is enough to have killed most of us sitting here, years ago. Red meat is awful. Soft drinks erode your stomach lining. Chinese food is loaded with MSG. Vegetables can be disastrous, and none of us realizes the long-term harm caused by the germs in our drinking water. But there is one food that is the most dangerous of all and we all have, or will, eat it. Can anyone here tell me what food it is that causes the most grief and suffering for years after eating it?"

Seamus O'Brien had been hailed as the most intelligent Irish man for three years running. He had topped such shows as Larry Gogans 'Just a Minute Quiz' and 'Quicksilver'. It was suggested by the Irish Mensa board that he should enter into the

English Mastermind Championships. He did, and won a place. On the evening of the competition, Seamus walks on stage, sits down and makes himself comfortable. The lights dim and a spotlight shines on his face. Magnus, the emcee, proceeds: "Seamus, what subject are you studying?" Seamus responds, "Irish history". "Very well," says Magnus, "your first question - in what year did the 'Easter Rising take place?" "Pass," says Seamus. "Okay," says Magnus, "Who was the leader of the Easter Rising?" Seamus responds,"Pass." "Well then," says Magnus, "how long did the Easter Rising last?" Again, Seamus responds, "Pass." Instantly, a voice from the audience shouts out: "Good man, Seamus - tell the English nothing..."

The teacher asked each of her students how they celebrated Christmas. She calls first on young Patrick O'Flaherty. "Tell me, Patrick, what do you do at Christmas time? Patrick addresses the class: "Me and my twelve brothers and sisters go to midnight Mass and we sing carols. Then we come home very late and we hang up our pillowcases at the foot of the bed. Then we go to bed and wait for Father Christmas to come with all our toys." "Very nice, Patrick," the teacher says. "Now, Billy Murphy, what do you do at Christmas?" "Me and my sister go to church with Mum and Dad, and we also sing carols. When we get home, we put biscuits and milk by the chimney and hang up our stockings. We hardly sleep waiting for Santa Claus to bring our presents." "That's also very nice, Billy," she said. Realizing that there was a Jewish boy in the class and not wanting to leave him out of the discussion, she asked him the same question. "Now, Isaac, what do you do at Christmas?" "Well, we also sing carols," Isaac responds. Surprised, the teacher questions further. "Tell us what you sing." "Well, it's the same thing every year. Dad comes home from the office. We all pile into the Rolls Royce and drive to his toy factory. When we get inside, we look at all the empty shelves and sing, 'What a friend we have in Jesus.' Then we all go to the Bahamas."

A passerby watched two Kerry men in a park. One was digging holes and the other was immediately filling them in again. "Tell me," said the passerby, "What on earth are you doing?" "Well," said the digger,"Usually there are three of us. I dig, Paddy plants the tree and Mick fills in the hole. Today Paddy is off ill, but that doesn't mean Mick and I get the day off, does it?"

Two Irish women walking through the forest one day hear a voice coming from near a log."Help me."

They lifted the log and underneath found a frog. "Help me " said the frog "I am an investment banker turned into a frog by an evil curse. I need to be kissed by a woman and I will turn back into an investment banker." One of the women grabbed the frog and stuffed it into her handbag. Aghast, her friend said, "Did you not hear the frog? He needs to to be returned to being an investment banker." "Listen", her friend said."these days a talking frog is worth a lot more than an investment banker."

Two English counterfeiters had produced thousands of genuine-looking notes - £50, £20, £10 - and really they should have been happy with their lot. Much wants more, so they scrambled through the discarded notes that had not passed close scrutiny. Among the jumble they came upon a perfectly fine note - watermarked, Queen's head in exactly the right place. The only trouble was that the amount shown was £18. Never mind,' said Brown, the bossman. "We'll unload it when we're over in Ireland." And so they took the note with them and, whilst in Kerry, they entered a corner shop to dispense with it "Excuse me," said Brown to shopkeeper Casey. "Have you got change for an £18 note?" "Indeed, sir," said Casey. "And would you like three sixes or two nines?"

When my wife's sister, Patty, was very young, she
was allowed to have her best friend, a boy named
Rory, over to spend the night. As the children grew
toward adolescence, their parents knew that
someday the sleepovers would have to end. One
night, when Rory and his family were visiting,
everyone gathered around the television to watch
the Rose of Tralee pageant. When Patty asked if
Rory could stay over, the parents hesitated,
wondering if the time had finally come to
discontinue the tradition. At that moment, the
pageant host announced a contestant's
measurements: 36-22-36. "Rory," his mother
asked, "what are those numbers?" The boy thought
for only a moment before responding, "Ninety-
four?"
Rory was allowed to stay.

For many years Kate Murphy had run the fruit and
vegetable stall in the town market and she'd
learned to have an answer for any situation. So
there she stood, watching the big Texan who was
poking around the stall. 'Hey, what are these?' he
asked. 'Apples,' said Kate. 'Apples?' laughed the
Yank. 'Why, in Texas we have apples twice that
size! And what are these?' "Those are potatoes,'
said Kate. 'Potatoes? Where I come from, bragged

the Texan, our potatoes are twice as big at least,'
Just then he picked up a cabbage, but before he
could speak Kate said: 'If you're not buying
Brussels sprouts, you'd best be putting that down.'

Sally was driving home from one of her business
trips in Northern Ireland when she saw an elderly
woman walking on the side of the road. As the trip
was a long and quiet one, she stopped the car and
asked the woman if she would like a ride. After a bit
of small talk and while resuming the journey the
woman noticed a brown bag on the seat next to
Sally. What's in the bag?" asked the woman. Sally
looked down at the brown bag and said, "It's a
bottle of wine, I got it for my husband." The woman
was silent for a moment. Then speaking with the
quiet wisdom of an elder she said: "Good trade."

A couple had two little boys, ages 8 and 10, who
were excessively mischievous. They were always
getting into trouble and their parents knew that, if
any mischief occurred in their village, their sons
were probably involved. The boys' mother heard
that the local vicar had been successful in
disciplining children, so she asked if he would
speak with her boys. The vicar agreed, but asked to
see them individually. So the mother sent her 8-

year-old in first that morning; with the older boy to
see the vicar in the afternoon. The vicar, a huge
man with a booming voice, sat the younger boy
down and asked him sternly, "Where is God?" The
boy's mouth dropped open, but he made no
response, sitting there with his mouth hanging
open, wide eyed. So the vicar repeated the question
in an even sterner tone, "Where is God!!?" Again
the boy made no attempt to answer. So the vicar
raised his voice even more and shook his finger in
the boy's face and bellowed, "WHERE IS GOD!!!!?"
The boy screamed and bolted from the room, ran
directly home and dived into a cupboard, slamming
the door behind him. When his older brother found
him in the cupboard , he asked, "What happened?"
The younger brother, gasping for breath, replied,
"We are in BIG trouble this time. God is missing -
and they think WE did it.!"

Sean got home in the early hours of the morning
after a night at the local pub. He made such a
racket as he weaved his way through the house that
he woke up the wife."By all the saints, what are you
doing down there?"she shouted from the bedroom.
"Get yourself up here and don't be waking the
neighbours." "I'm trying to get a barrel of Guinness
up the stairs," he shouted back. "Leave it 'till the
morning," she shouted down. "I can't" says he, "I've
drank it!"

Two nearby castles are at war. One shoots a cannonball at the other. Bang. A piece of wall breaks. In a while the second castle shoots at the first one. A part of a tower becomes a pile of stones. And so on for some time. Then there is a long silence. Suddenly from one of the castles a cry is heard: "Why don't you shoot?" And the answer: "You have the cannonball."

A Jesuit priest decided to visit a small island off the coast of Connemara. The inhabitants numbered no more than a couple of dozen, but the priest threw himself into the Lord's work with a vengeance. Having taken over the bar of the pub for Mass, and having delivered a fire and brimstone sermon, he questioned his small congregation. "How long is it since any of you had your confessions heard?" he asked. "Well, Father,' answered Brendan, the oldest inhabitant. "It must be three years since the last priest was here." "Why didn't you make a trip to the mainland?" thundered the priest. "Well, Father,' said Brendan, "the water between us and the mainland is very rough, and our boat is old and leaky. So you see. if we've only venial sins to confess, it's not worth the bother, and if we've mortal sins, it's not worth the risk!"

A minister dies and is waiting in line at the Pearly Gates. Ahead of him is a lad dressed in sunglasses, loud shirt, leather jacket, and jeans. Saint Peter addresses the lad: "Who are you, so that I may know whether or not to admit you to the Kingdom of Heaven?" The fellah replies, "I'm Johnny O'Rourke, taxi-driver, Brooklyn, New York." Saint Peter consults his list. He smiles and says to the taxi-driver, "Take this silken robe and golden staff and enter the Kingdom of Heaven." The taxi-driver goes into Heaven with his robe and staff, and it's the minister's turn. He stands erect and booms out, "I am Phillip Smith, pastor of Saint Mary's for the last forty-three years." Saint Peter consults his list. He says to the minister, "Take this cotton robe and wooden staff and enter the Kingdom of Heaven." "Just a minute," says the minister. "That man was a taxi-driver and he gets a silken robe and golden staff. How can this be?" "Up here, we work by results," says Saint Peter. "While you preached, people slept; while he drove, people prayed."

An attractive young lady was on a plane arriving from Ireland. She found herself seated next to an elderly priest whom she asked: "Excuse me Father, could I ask a favor?" "Of course my child, What can

I do for you?" "Here is the problem.I bought myself a new sophisticated vibrating hair remover for which I paid an enormous sum of money. I have really gone over the declaration limits and I am worried that they will confiscate it at customs. Do you think you could hide it under your cassock?" "Of course I could, my child, but you must realize that I cannot lie." "You have such an honest face Father, I am sure they will not ask you any questions", and she gave him the worrisome personal gadget. The aircraft arrived at its destination. When the priest presented himself to customs he was asked, "Father, do you have anything to declare?" "From the top of my head to my sash, I have nothing to declare, my son", he replied. Finding his reply strange, the customs officer asked, "And from the sash down, what do you have?" The priest replied, "I have there a marvelous little instrument destined for use by women, but which has never been used." Breaking out in laughter, the customs officer said, "Go ahead Father. Next!"

A minister was completing a temperance sermon. With great emphasis he said, "If I had all the beer in the world, I'd take it and pour it into the river." With even greater emphasis he said, "And if I had all the wine in the world, I'd take it and pour it into the river." And then finally, shaking his fist in the air, he said, "And if I had all the whiskey in the world,I'd take it and pour it into the river." Sermon complete, he then sat down. The choir director stood very cautiously and announced with a smile, for our closing selection,let us sing Hymn #365, "Shall We Gather at the River."

Father Murphy walks into a pub in Donegal, and asks the first man he meets, 'Do you want to go to heaven?'
The man said, 'I do, Father.'
The priest said, 'Then stand over there against the wall.'
Then the priest asked the second man, 'Do you want to go to heaven?'
'Certainly, Father,' the man replied.
'Then stand over there against the wall,' said the priest.
Then Father Murphy walked up to O'Toole and asked, 'Do you want to go to heaven?'
O'Toole said, 'No, I don't Father.'
The priest said, 'I don't believe this. You mean to tell me that when you die you don't want to go to heaven?'
O'Toole said, 'Oh, when I die , yes. I thought you were getting a group together to go right now.'

Paddy was in New York. He was patiently waiting and watching the traffic cop on a busy street crossing. The cop stopped the flow of traffic and shouted, 'Okay, pedestrians.' Then he'd allow the traffic to pass. He'd done this several times, and Paddy still stood on the sidewalk. After the cop had shouted, 'Pedestrians!' for the tenth time, Paddy went over to him and said, 'Is it not about time ye let the Catholics across?'

Gallagher opened the morning newspaper and was dumbfounded to read in the obituary column that he had died. He quickly phoned his best friend, Finney.
'Did you see the paper?' asked Gallagher. 'They say I died!!'
'Yes, I saw it!' replied Finney. 'Where are ye callin' from?'

Joey-Jim was tooling along the road one fine day when the local policeman, a friend of his, pulled him over. "What's wrong, Seamus?" Joey-Jim asked. "Well didn't ya know, Joey-Jim, that your wife fell out of the car about five miles back?" said Seamus. "Ah, praise the Almighty!" he replied with relief. "I thought I'd gone deaf

An Irish priest is driving down to New York and gets stopped for speeding in Connecticut . The state trooper smells alcohol on the priest's breath and then sees an empty wine bottle on the floor of the car.

He says, 'Sir, have you been drinking?'

'Just water,' says the priest.

The trooper says, 'Then why do I smell wine?'

The priest looks at the bottle and says, 'Good Lord! He's done it again!'

Paddy was driving down the street in a sweat because he had an important meeting and couldn't find a parking place. Looking up to heaven he said, 'Lord take pity on me. If you find me a parking place I will go to Mass every Sunday for the rest of me life and give up me Irish Whiskey!'

Miraculously, a parking place appeared.

Paddy looked up again and said, 'Never mind, I found one.'

Three Irishman are drinking at a bar. he first says: "Aye, this is a nice bar, but where I come from, there's a better one. At MacDougal's, you buy a drink, you buy another drink, and MacDougal himself will buy your third drink!"

The second then starts: "That sounds like a nice bar, but where I come from, there's a better one called Quinns. At Quinns, you buy a drink, Quinn buys you a drink. You buy another drink, Quinn buys you another drink."

Then the third pipes up. "You think that's good? Where I come from, there's this place called Murphy's. At Murphy's, they buy you your first drink, they buy you your second drink, they buy you your third drink, and then, they take you in the back and get you laid!"

"Wow!" say the other two. "That sounds fantastic! Did that actually happen to you?" "No," replies their friend, "but it happened to my sister!"

Walking into the bar, Mike said to Charlie the bartender, 'Pour me a stiff one - just had another fight with the little woman.'

'Oh yeah?' said Charlie, 'And how did this one end?'

'When it was over,' Mike replied, 'She came to me on her hands and knees.'

'Really,' said Charles, 'Now that's a switch! What did she say?'

She said, 'Come out from under the bed, you little chicken.'

Paddy had been drinking at his local Dublin pub all day and most of the night celebrating St Patrick's Day. Mick, the bartender, finally says, "You'll not be drinking any more tonight, Paddy."

Paddy replies, "OK Mick, I'll be on my way then."Paddy spins around on his stool and steps off. He falls flat on his face."Shoite," he says and pulls himself up by the stool and dusts himself off. He takes a step towards the door and falls flat on his face again, "Shoite, Shoite!"

He looks to the doorway and thinks to himself that if he can just get to the door and some fresh air he'll be fine. He belly crawls to the door and shimmies up to the door frame. He sticks his head outside and takes a deep breath of fresh air, feels much better, and takes a step out onto the sidewalk and falls flat on his face."Bi'Jesus.... I'm fockin ' focked," he says.

He can see his house just a few doors down, and crawls to the door, hauls himself up the door frame, opens the door and goes inside. He takes a look up the stairs and says, "No fockin' way." He crawls up the stairs to his bedroom door and says. "I can make it to the bed." He takes a step into the room and falls flat on his face.

He says "Fock it" and falls into bed.The next morning, his wife, Jess, comes into the room carrying a cup of coffee and says, "Get up Paddy. Did you have a bit to drink last night?"

Paddy says, "I did, Jess. I was fockin' pissed. But how did you know?"

"Mick phoned... you left your wheelchair at the pub."

Scorcher Murphy was selling his house, and put the matter in an agent's hands. The agent wrote up a sales blurb for the house that made wonderful reading. After Murphy read it, he turned to the agent and asked,"Have I got all ye say there?"The agent said, "Certainly ye have...Why d'ye ask?"Replied Murphy, "Cancel the sale...'tis too good to part with."

Shamus and Murphy fancied a pint or two but didn't have a lot of money between them, they could only raise the staggering sum of one Euro. Murphy said "Hang on, I have an idea."

He went next door to the butcher's shop and came out with one large sausage.

Shamus said "Are you crazy? Now we don't have any money left at all!"

Murphy replied, "Don't worry - just follow me."

He went into the pub where he immediately ordered two pints of Guinness and two glasses of Jamieson Whisky.

Shamus said "Now you've lost it. Do you know how much trouble we will be in? We haven't got any money!!"

Murphy replied, with a smile. "Don't worry, I have a plan, Cheers!"

They downed their Drinks. Murphy said, "OK, I'll stick the sausage through my zipper and you go on your knees and put it in your mouth."

The barman noticed them, went berserk, and threw them out.

They continued this, pub after pub, getting more and more drunk, all for free..

At the tenth pub Shamus said "Murphy - I don't think I can do any more of this. I'm drunk and me knees are killin' me!"

Murphy said, "How do you think I feel? I lost the sausage in the third pub".

An Irishman, is stumbling through the woods, totally drunk, when he comes upon a preacher baptising people in the river.

He proceeds to walk into the water and subsequently bumps into the preacher.

The preacher turns around and is almost overcome by the smell of alcohol, whereupon he asks the drunk,

'Are you ready to find Jesus?'

The drunk shouts, 'Yes, oi am.'

So the preacher grabs him and dunks him in the water.

He pulls him up and asks the drunk, 'Brother have you found Jesus?'

The drunk replies, 'No, oi haven't found Jesus.'
The preacher shocked at the answer, dunks him into the water again for a little longer.
He again pulls him out of the water and asks again, 'Have you found Jesus me brother?'
The drunk again answers, 'No,oi I haven't found Jesus.'
By this time the preacher is at his wits end and dunks the drunk in the water again —
but this time holds him down for about 30 seconds and when he begins kicking his arms and legs he pulls him up.
The preacher again asks the drunk, 'For the love of God have you found Jesus yet.?'
The Drunk wipes his eyes and catches his breath and says to the preacher 'Are ya sure dis is where he fell in?'

What did the Irishman call a Pakistani cloakroom attendant?
Mahatma Coat

A 54 year old Irish women woman had a heart attack and was taken to the hospital in Dublin.
While on the operating table she had a near death experience.
Seeing God she asked "Is my time up?"

God said, "No, you have another 43 years, 2 months and 8 days to live."

Upon recovery, the woman decided to stay in the hospital and have a face-lift, liposuction, breast implants and a tummy tuck. She even had someone come in and change her hair color and brighten her teeth!

Since she had so much more time to live, she figured she might as well make the most of it. After her last operation, she was released from the hospital.

While crossing the street on her way home, she was killed by an ambulance..

Arriving in front of God, she demanded, "I thought you said I had another 43 years. Why didn't you pull me from out of the path of the ambulance?"

God replied:

"I didn't recognize you!"

An English builder is keen to implement the EU's policy of job mobility, so he advertises a job in an international trade paper. Three applicants turn up: a Frenchman, a German and an Irishman. When the builder interviews them he points out that a basic knowledge of English is essential, especially of terms used in the building trade, so he has devised a little test. He asks each one of them the same question: " Can you explain to me the difference between 'girder' and 'joist'?"

The Frenchman shrugs his shoulders, admitting that he does not understand the terms. The German also admits that he has no idea.
Before the builder puts the question to the Irishman, he says "I know you speak English, but in the interests of equal treatment I have to ask you the same question as the other two: "What is the difference between 'girder' and 'joist'?"
The Irishman replies, "Sure, everyone knows that. Goethe wrote 'Faust' and Joyce wrote 'Ulysses'."

Two attorneys went into a diner and ordered two drinks. Then they produced sandwiches from their briefcases and started to eat. The owner became quite concerned and marched over and told them, "You can't eat your own sandwiches in here!"
The attorneys looked at each other, shrugged their shoulders and then exchanged sandwiches.

A pompous priest was seated next to an Irishman on a flight home. After the plane was airborne, drink orders were taken. The Irishman asked for an Irish whiskey. The attendant placed the drink on his tray and then asked the priest if he would like a drink. He replied in disgust," I'd rather be savagely ravaged by brazen hussies than let alcohol touch my lips."The Irishman then handed his drink back to the attendant and said "Me too. I didn't know we had a choice!"

Donavan, while visiting Italy, met a sailor from Venice. Before long they found themselves in a tavern. After several hours of heavy drinking the Italian finally slid under the table. The Irishman staggered to his feet and announced, "I'm the first guy who ever drank a Venetian blind!"

An Irishman and an Englishman are hunting out in the woods when the Englishman falls to the ground. He doesn't seem to be breathing, his eyes are rolled back in his head. The Irishman whips out his phone and calls the emergency services. He gasps to the operator: "My friend is dead! What can I do?" The operator, in a calm soothing voice says: "Just take it easy. I can help. First, let's make sure he's dead." There is a silence, then a shot is heard. The man's voice comes back on the line. He says: "OK, now what?"

"I hear Murphy died," said Pat. "Was he ill long?""No," said Mick. "He died in the best of health."

Mick met Paddy in the street and said, 'Paddy, will you draw your bedroom curtains before making love to your wife in future?'
'Bejaysus Why?' Paddy asked.
'Because,' said Mick, 'The whole street was laughing when they saw you
and your missus making love yesterday.'
Paddy said, 'Stupid bastards, the laugh's on them ... I wasn't home yesterday.'

Murphy lay in hospital covered in bandages head to foot - with just two little slits for his eyes. 'What happened to you?' asked Cassidy.
'I staggered out of the pub and a lorry hit me a glancing blow and knocked me through a plate glass window.'
'Begod,' said Cassidy. 'It's a good job you were wearing those bandages or you'd have been cut to ribbons!'

Paddy calls EasyJet to book a flight. The operator asks "How many people are flying with you?" Paddy replies "I don't know! It's your airline!" Two Irish couples decided to swap partners for the night. After 3 hours of passionate sex Paddy asks "I wonder how the girls are getting on?"

Paddy takes his new wife to bed on their wedding night. She undresses and lays on the bed spread-eagled and asks "You know what I want don't you?" "Yeah," says Paddy "the whole friggin bed by the looks of it!"

Paddy & his wife are lying in bed and the neighbour's dog is barking like mad in the next door garden. Paddy says "To hell with this!" and storms off. He returns five minutes later and the dog is still barking and his wife asks "What did you do?" Paddy replies "I've put the dog in our garden, let's see how they like it!"

Mick & Paddy are reading head stones at a nearby cemetery. Mick say "Crikey! There's a bloke here who was 152!" Paddy asks "What was his name?"

Mick replies "Miles from London!"

Murphy was driving limo in New York and one day he picks up the Pope at Kennedy airport. The Pope tells the Murphy "I like these big cars...you mind if I drive?" So Murphy jumps in the back seat and lets the Pope drive into the city. He gets pulled over by Sullivan the cop who radios his captain and says "I just pulled over a really important guy."
 Captain says, "Who is it? The Mayor?"
   Sullivan says, "Bigger than that. He's got the Pope driving for him."

An American tourist was driving in County Kerry, when his motor stopped. He got out to see if he could locate the trouble. A voice behind him said, "The trouble is the carburetor."
He turned around and only saw an old horse. The horse said again, "It's the carburetor that's not working."
The American nearly died with fright, and dashed into the nearest pub, had a large whiskey, and told Murphy the bartender what the horse had said to him.
Murphy said, "Well, don't pay any attention to him, he knows nothing about cars anyway."

In London a homeless Irishman walks up to a proper Englishman and asks for some spare change. The Englishman says "Neither a borrower nor a lender be. Shakespeare."
The Irishman man says, "Fuck you. Brendan Behan"

A man comes home early and finds Murphy naked, hiding behind the shower curtain.
"What are you doing in there?"
"Voting." Murphy says

A Kerry man went for a job at the local stables and the farmer said "Can you shoe horses?" The Kerry man thinks for a minute and then says "No, but I once told a donkey to get lost."

An elderly Kerry couple is sitting together watching television. During one of 'those' commercials, the husband asked his wife, "Whatever happened to our sexual relations?" After a long thoughtful silence, the wife replied, "You know, I don't know. I don't even think we got a Christmas card from them this year.

While impatiently waiting for a table in a restaurant, Miss O'Leary says to Mrs. Clancy, "If they weren't so crowded in here all the time, they'd do a lot more business

An Irish daughter had not been home for over 5 years.
Upon her return, her Father cussed her.
"Where have ye been all this time? Why did ye not write to us, not even a line?"
"Why didn't ye call? Can ye not understand what ye put yer old Mother thru?"
The girl, crying, replied, "Sniff, sniff....Dad....I became a prostitute..."
"Ye what!!? Out of here, ye shameless harlot! Sinner! You're a disgrace to this Catholic family."
"OK, Dad-- as ye wish."
"I just came back to give mum this luxurious fur coat, title deed to a ten bedroom mansion plus a $5 million savings certificate."
"For me little brother, this gold Rolex."

"And for ye Daddy, the sparkling new Mercedes limited edition convertible that's parked outside plus a membership to the country club..............
(takes a breath)............. and an invitation for ye all to spend New Year's Eve on board my new yacht in the Riviera and....."

"Now what was it ye said ye had become?" says Dad.

Girl, crying again, "Sniff, sniff....a prostitute Daddy! Sniff, sniff."

"Oh! Be Jesus! Ye scared me half to death, girl!"

"I thought ye said a Protestant, come here and give yer old Dad a hug."

It's Christmas time and Paddy and Sean decide to go look for a Christmas Tree. They gather their axe, a sled, and a broom to brush the trees off so they can get a good look at them.

When they finally reach a fine group of trees, Sean brushes off the first tree, and stands back with Paddy to look at it. "Well, Paddy, What do you think?"

"Sorry, Sean, this tree won't do. Let's try another one."

They come upon another nice tree, Sean brushes it off, and they both look at it. "How about this one, Paddy?"

"Not quite, Sean. Let's keep looking."

This goes on until nightfall. Both Paddy and Sean are cold, tired, and hungry. "Well, Paddy, what do we do now?"
"Sean, I think we should take home the next tree we find, whether it has lights on it or not..."

#####

16399700R00099

Made in the USA
Middletown, DE
13 December 2014